Gunpowder on Their Skirts

Gunpowder on Their Skirts

MILITARY HEROINES FOR THE BLUE AND GRAY

WRITTEN AND ILLUSTRATED BY STEPHANIE H. FORD

PELICAN PUBLISHING COMPANY
GRETNA 2018

Library of Congress Cataloging-in-Publication Data

Names: Ford, Stephanie (Stephanie H.), author, illustrator.
Title: Gunpowder on their skirts : military heroines for the blue and gray / written and illustrated by Stephanie H. Ford.
Description: Gretna : Pelican Publishing Company, 2018. | Audience: 009-013. | Audience: 004-006. | Includes bibliographical references and index. Identifiers: LCCN 2018023954| ISBN 9781455624355 (paperback : alk. paper) | ISBN 9781455624362 (ebook)
Subjects: LCSH: United States—History—Civil War, 1861-1865—Participation, Female—Juvenile literature. | United States—History—Civil War, 1861-1865—Women—Juvenile literature. | United States—History—Civil War, 1861-1865—Biography—Juvenile literature. | Women— United States—Biography—Juvenile literature. | Women—United States—History—19th century—Juvenile literature. | LCGFT: Biographies.
Classification: LCC E628 .F68 2018 | DDC 973.7082—dc23 LC record available at https://lccn.loc.gov/2018023954

Frontispiece: A romanticized depiction of Annie Etheridge in battle. (*Women's Work in the War,* 1867)

Printed in the United States of America
Published by Pelican Publishing Company, Inc.
1000 Burmaster Street, Gretna, Louisiana 70053
www.pelicanpub.com

To Sadie:
"Be on your guard; stand firm in the faith;
be courageous; be strong."

Contents

Acknowledgments 9
Introduction 11

Part I: Women for the Blue: Fighting to Preserve the Union
Chapter 1: Kady Brownell 15
Chapter 2: Annie Etheridge 20
Chapter 3: Susie Baker 26
Chapter 4: Mary Tepe 30
Chapter 5: Dr. Mary Walker 36
Chapter 6: Bridget Divers 41

Part II: Women for the Gray: Fighting for Southern Independence
Chapter 7: Capt. Sally Tompkins 48
Chapter 8: Nancy Hart 52
Chapter 9: Mary Sophia Hill 55
Chapter 10: Sindy Riller Boles 61
Chapter 11: Lucy Ann Cox 64
Chapter 12: Oriana Moon 69
Chapter 13: Betsy Sullivan 74
Chapter 14: Rose K. Rooney 79

Women on Battlefields: A History 82
Glossary 86
Notes 90
Bibliography 93
Index 96

Acknowledgments

Research for *Gunpowder on Their Skirts* began many years ago when I read my first account of a **vivandière** and decided I wanted to portray one at historical reenactments. At the time, material about these brave young women who provided support to troops on nineteenth-century battlefields was much more difficult to come by. Since then several titles have been published on the subject of women's military roles during the **Civil War/War Between the States**, but these modern works give the bulk of the attention to women who disguised themselves as men. Those women who abandoned their female identities in order to fight did not hold my interest or stir my imagination. I wanted to focus on the women who ventured onto the battlefields wearing skirts.

I decided to write this book for a younger audience as it is with the next generation that we leave our precious history. To complete this work, I had help from many individuals: Kathey Hunt, who introduced me to Sindy Riller Boles and directed me to the Kaufman County Commissioners Court Minutes where her story was buried; Hugh McLauren, who shared his discovery of Rebecca Sineath; Teresa Roane, who listened to my questions about minority women who served in the war and shared the existence of Julia Mason; The Pearce Museum in Corsicana, Texas, for allowing me to use their resources; my husband, who offered unfailing support and helped sift through muster cards and rosters on Fold3; and my daughter, who suffered through my hours on the computer and the phone and through trips to battlefields, libraries, and archives. Thank you to my editors, Nina Kooij and Lindsey Reynolds, for their support, to Antoinette de Alteriis for encouraging me on this particular book, and to several others at Pelican Publishing Company. Lastly, I want to thank all those in the living history community who have supported my role as a vivandière in order to better understand these women. Due to their belief in what I was doing, I am able to tell these women's stories with a conviction I do not believe would otherwise be possible.

Introduction

Much has been written about the fighting men of the **Civil War/ War Between the States** (1861-1865), and recently there has been a push to balance the story of the men with stories of women who made contributions to the effort. Those women who cut their hair, bound their breasts, and disguised themselves as men to fight alongside their male comrades have received the most attention. However, I wondered whether a woman had to dress like a man in the 1860s to possess more than a secondary role in the war—one where she could be considered a soldier, even if in an **auxiliary** position similar to our modern medics, engineers, and mechanics. Were there women who contributed in ways other than nursing wounded men in hospitals far removed from the front line of battle, women who actually stepped onto the battlefields without having to hide their gender? The answer is yes! There were such women. Many such women! More than I could ever mention here.

Unfortunately, most of the stories I uncovered were small side notes made in records or soldiers' journals and did not contain enough information to piece together a complete biography. Those mentions did reveal just how common a woman's presence was in the armies of the blue and the gray. In this book, I focus upon the stories of the women for whom I did uncover enough information for their complete stories to be told. I'll also note that I tried to be balanced and fair in the telling of these women's stories, avoiding **presentism** when trying to understand them. There are many aspects of nineteenth-century American culture that are difficult for us in the twenty-first century to comprehend—even after decades of study.

I also tried to represent an equal number of women on each side of the conflict, but ultimately more Confederate women found their way into this book. The reasons for this are twofold: First, immediately after the war, the South had to focus on mere survival and rebuilding while those in the North had the opportunity to sit down and write books. One was Frank Moore's *Women of the War,* published just one year after Appomattox. Moore writes only of Northern women. Their stories, because of his book, are better known in the historical community. I included a few Northern women from Moore's book who best fit the type of women I wanted to feature, but I chose to focus my energy on lesser known women. Secondly, except for Gettysburg and a few towns in Ohio, the war was fought almost exclusively in the South. If women in the North wished to go to the front lines to help, they had to travel. Their government was also not as open to accepting their help as the Confederate government in the South. Southern women, by contrast, saw the battles come right to their doorstep.

Ultimately, whether the women I've written about threw their lot in with the Union or the Confederate cause, they were women who were proud to be women and did not let go of their femininity nor allow it to stop them from taking an active role in the war that rumbled into their lives. They were women who were not afraid to get gunpowder on their skirts.

Part 1

Women for the Blue

FIGHTING TO PRESERVE THE UNION

Patriotic image from the war. (Library of Congress)

Chapter 1

Kady Brownell

Color-Bearer for Rhode Island

Kady Southwell was born in 1842 in South Africa, far away from America. During that time, the Xhosa Wars were raging. Her father was a colonel in the British army, and her mother had followed him to war. According to legend, her mother arrived to a battlefield near Caffara, and as she watched the frenzy of battle, she went into labor. Kady was born there on the battlefield.[1] While the detail of her birth on the battlefield is presumably the creation of the press, it was symbolic of how the military image would come to define much of Kady's identity.

Her mother died shortly after Kady was born, so while other girls her age were playing with tea sets and dolls, Kady was allowed to follow her father to work. She learned how to ride horses, use a sword, and fire a rifle. After a time, Kady's father thought it best for his daughter to grow up in a nice home and learn needlework and music rather than military drills, and she was sent to live with relatives near Providence, Rhode Island.

In her new home, Kady was expected to go to school, wear pretty dresses with many petticoats, polish her manners, and act the way a proper young Victorian lady should. However, Kady's early childhood in the military barracks in a faraway land made her long for adventure.

In March of 1861, Kady fell in love with a young miller named Robert Brownell. They soon married, and a life at home making meals, entertaining guests, and raising children appeared to be in her future, but only a month into their marriage the drums of war sounded. Robert immediately volunteered to be a soldier. Seeing her chance for adventure and not wanting to be separated from her new husband, Kady chose to join him when he enlisted. As women were not allowed to be soldiers, Kady chose to be a nurse and was adopted as the mascot of her husband's regiment.

Unfortunately, when the regiment was heading to war, a high-ranking officer came to her and said, "Women are not allowed here. Go home!" Kady was extremely unhappy and did not want to return home. Determined not to be left behind, she contacted the governor of Rhode Island, who gave her special permission to be the First Rhode Island's official **daughter of the regiment.** With the governor's special order clutched in her hand, Kady left for war.[2]

Armed with a sword and a rifle, Kady was allowed to be the regiment's **color-bearer.** Those early months of the war saw quite a few daughters of the regiment, and they, like the men, wore bright uniforms. No one thought the war would last long. Everyone thought it would be a time for the men to show how brave they could be, and then they'd come home to an adoring public. Few thought of how dangerous war really was. They only saw the bright uniforms and pretty silk flags and listened to the brass bands as if it were all a big celebration. How soon they were proven wrong!

Kady carried the regiment's flag at the first battle of the war, Bull Run, in Virginia. It was a horrible battle for the Union troops, and the First Rhode Island tasted defeat. In fact, the battle went so horribly wrong that Kady was slightly wounded in the foot from a bullet. She had to wrap a bandage around her wound and run along with her husband all the way back to **Washington City.**[3]

After discovering that color-bearer was a dangerous job, the men of Kady's regiment decided that from then on Kady had to give up the flag just before the charge was sounded. Instead, she was to remain behind and help the wounded. For over a year, Kady marched with the soldiers of her regiment and cared for them in camp.

In 1862, Kady's regiment was fighting in the battle at New Bern when they spotted a large group of soldiers through the trees. There was so much smoke that no one could tell if they were fellow Union soldiers or Confederates. Suddenly, Kady recognized them as Northern fighters, but they were about to fire their rifles upon the First Rhode Island. The officers and men shouted that they were friends, not the enemy, but the battle was too loud and their voices were swallowed in the din. The other Union soldiers began to fire and Kady began to see her comrades fall from the friendly fire.

Fast-thinking Kady knew what needed to be done. She raced from the rear of the line, snatched the colors, and ran between the lines.

Kady Brownell poses for a photograph after arriving home from the war. (Library of Congress)

There she waved the flag, letting the other soldiers know not to fire.[4] Kady was declared a hero.

Unfortunately, later in that battle, Robert was badly wounded. He would never fight again and Kady decided her first duty was to her husband and so she returned home.

For the rest of the war, after her husband was well enough to travel, they visited cities all over the North to drum up support for the war. They helped raise money and urged people to donate supplies. They even convinced some young men to enlist to fight. Due to these efforts, Kady was photographed in her vivandière uniform time and again, becoming the most photographed woman of the war.

A fashion plate from 1860 showing clothing popular during Kady's time. (*Godey's*, August 1860)

What was expected of girls in 1861?

Girls were expected to be quiet, timid, and caring. They usually only attended school until the eighth grade. In addition to learning to read and write, they learned music, embroidery, and beautiful handwriting. All girls were expected to wear dresses with layers of petticoats, hoops, and even corsets from an early age.

What was a color-bearer?

A color-bearer was someone chosen to carry the regiment's flag. It was a position of great honor but also a dangerous place on the battlefield. Flags were used as a guidepost for troops in the confusion of battle, showing them where their regiment was located. It also reminded them of what they were fighting for. Enemy soldiers would try to shoot the color-bearer in order to cause confusion. Great honor was gained in capturing the enemy's colors.

A photograph of a Pennsylvania color-bearer during the war showing off his regiment's torn, battle-worn flag. (Library of Congress)

Chapter 2

Annie Etheridge

Michigan's Brave Daughter

Anna Etheridge, or "Annie," had a difficult childhood. She was born into a wealthy household but her family quickly lost everything. Her fine dresses and nice toys were sold so her family could have enough food, and her family was forced to move from house to house throughout the states of Michigan and Wisconsin. Annie learned at a young age that the important things in life are not things you can buy; instead, the greatest value can be found in helping others. It was the joy she found in lending aid that made her decide to follow her new husband to war in 1861.

Many men thought being a soldier would be fun, an adventure where they could prove how brave they were. But being a soldier was hard. Soldiers slept outside, in tents if they were lucky. They camped in hot weather and in cold, when it was raining and when it was windy. They ate the same food day after day and had to walk until their feet were covered in blisters and then they had to march some more. Annie's husband quickly decided he didn't want to be a soldier, and he told Annie he wanted to **desert.** Annie didn't wish to run away and abandon the soldiers so she firmly decided to stay. Her determination was not enough to convince her husband to do the same, so he left her and the army, sneaking away in the middle of the night.

Now alone in the army, Annie wondered if she would be allowed to stay because one of the rules required of a woman to follow a regiment was that she be married. Luckily, the Third Michigan Volunteer

Infantry Regiment knew what had happened and loved Annie's loyalty to the soldiers and her patriotism. They gladly welcomed her, and she left for Virginia alongside them with a pack full of medicine.

She wore only a simple skirt and blouse and marched with the men. When the men were engaged in battle, she would hang back at the rear of the line. When a man was wounded, she would rush forward to mend his wounds and then help him behind the battle line to where he could be taken to a field hospital.

In 1862, Annie was working through fierce fighting at the Second Battle of Bull Run, when the soldiers began to retreat. She was nearly captured by enemy soldiers. Gen. Philip Kearny rode up and found her kneeling by a wounded soldier, helplessly looking on as the gray line of Confederate soldiers drew closer. He pulled her onto his horse and helped her escape. After the ordeal, General Kearny ordered that a horse be provided for Annie so she could do her work more safely. Kearny was so impressed with how bravely she worked, despite being in danger, that he awarded her a medal called the Kearny Cross.[1]

Annie helped wounded soldiers in many battles of the war, including Bull Run, Antietam, and Fredericksburg, where while she was tending a wounded man on the field, a cannon shell burst nearby, killing the soldier she was tending and tearing a large hole in her skirt![2] At Chancellorsville, in May of 1863, Annie was struck in the hand by a bullet, but her injury did not stop her from performing her duty as a nurse on the battlefield. She continued helping soldiers during the battles at Gettysburg and Spotsylvania Court House. Twice she had to find a new horse as hers were killed during battles. Many soldiers wrote home about her bravery, courage, and how much love she must have had for the soldiers in order for her to endure such harsh situations.

Even though Annie did so much for the soldiers, in 1864, Gen. Ulysses S. Grant passed an order that said all women who were travelling with the army had to go home. Annie's soldiers pleaded with General Grant to let her stay, but he refused to make an exception and Annie had to leave.[3] Not ready to return home, she decided to help in a large hospital in a city. While her days of tending to wounded men on the battlefields and in the soldiers' camps were over, she still found a way to help them until the end of the war.

Annie Etheridge, most likely during the war, wearing the Kearny Cross. (Michael J. McAfee Collection)

US
US

Annie during or immediately after the war. (Foard Collection of Civil War Nursing)

What's in a name?

As battles are mentioned in this book, the names favored by the Union side are used when talking about Union women, and names favored by the Confederates are used when discussing Confederate women. The Union named battles after rivers and streams while the Confederates named them after the closest town. The most well-known battles include:

Union	**Confederate**
Bull Run	Manassas
Antietam	Sharpsburg
Pittsburg Landing	Shiloh
Stones River	Mufreesboro

Annie tending to the wounded during the Second Battle of Bull Run.

What happened to a soldier who was wounded?

A soldier who was wounded on the battlefield usually had to tend to himself. If he was lucky, a nurse like Annie would be there to help him. After he was quickly bandaged, he would be sent to a makeshift hospital in a house or tent close to the fighting. This was called a **field hospital.** After seeing a surgeon at a field hospital, if a soldier still needed care, he would be sent to a large hospital in a major city. Many women volunteered to be nurses and helped at the large **military hospitals** in the cities, far away from the battlefields. Dorothea Dix, Mary Ann Bickerdyke, and Louisa May Alcott—author of *Little Women*—are among the most well-known Northern women to have served as nurses in Civil War hospitals. The most famous of all is Clara Barton, who worked in both military hospitals and field hospitals and went on to found the American Red Cross.

Dorothea Dix, head of nursing for the Union. (Library of Congress)

Reproduction of a Civil War-era ambulance. (Photo by the author)

Hospital Flags, 1861-1865

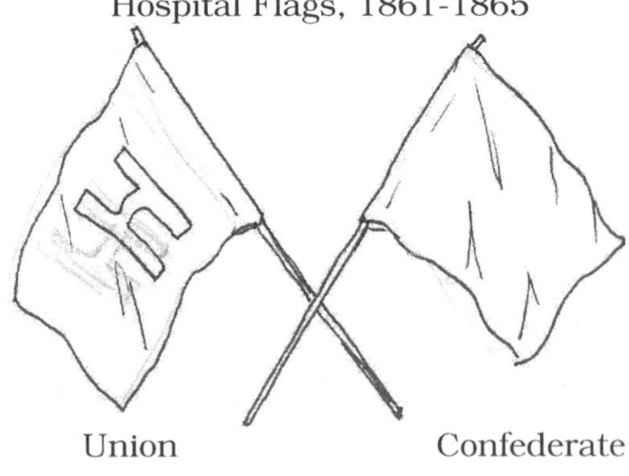

A Taste of History

What did Union soldiers eat? Most soldiers received a ration of salted pork, coffee, sugar, and hard biscuits called **hardtack** that looked like large crackers. At times, they received canned goods, which were a new invention, and these may have contained vegetables, oysters, or condensed milk.

To taste a bit of history yourself, you can make hardtack crackers just like the soldiers ate by using this recipe:

Ingredients
4 cups flour
1 cup water
4 tsp. salt

Preheat oven to 250 degrees. In a large bowl, mix together all ingredients until dough is no longer sticky. Add more flour or more water if necessary to achieve the proper texture. Form dough into a ball and then roll out onto a floured surface with a rolling pin until dough is approximately ⅓-½-inch thick. Using a knife or pizza cutter, cut dough into three-inch squares. Place squares onto a cookie tray covered with parchment paper. Poke a grid of holes in the top of the squares with a toothpick. Place in oven and cook for four hours. Once done, cool on rack.

To properly make hardtack, all the moisture must be baked out of the dough as it cooks. If you bake the dough faster at higher temperatures, it will not be as hard as the soldiers experienced.

Caution: Crackers will be hard and will harden more over time! If kept dry, the crackers will last indefinitely. It is suggested the crackers be soaked or broken with a mallet before eating. A common way for the soldiers to eat the crackers would be to soak them in their coffee or break them apart with the butt of their muskets and add them to pork fat in a skillet.

Hardtack on a military cracker box. (Photo by the author)

Chapter 3

Susie Baker

Nurse and Teacher

One dark night in 1862, Susie Baker was moving in secret. For weeks, cannon shells had been falling around her home near Savannah, Georgia. Fearing for her life, Susie agreed to escape with her uncle and his family. Another reason she travelled so quietly was that when she reached the Union lines, she would no longer be a slave.

Freedom, however, was not what Susie expected. In fact, Susie began to wonder if she had traded one form of slavery for another. The Union army forced her uncle and male cousins to be soldiers. And since they were "colored" soldiers, they were made to do jobs the white Union soldiers didn't want to do, such as chop down trees to make roads, dig trenches and **latrines,** and bury horses and mules that died. They forced Susie to do laundry. She was made to spend long days washing socks and dirty shirts in big wooden tubs filled with lye soap that made her hands rough and dry. It was a long process of scrubbing and squeezing, drying and folding, and boiling large pots of water even on the hottest days. Susie had wanted so much more. Her life as a slave hadn't been like some. She wasn't use to this sort of work.

At a young age, Susie was seen to be kind and smart, so her master sent her to the city of Savannah to live with a woman who had once been his slave but was now free. While there, Susie attended school. She knew she was lucky and focused on being an excellent student. When she had learned all she could, a friend, a young man, agreed to teach her more.[1] When war was declared in April of 1861, Susie's new teacher had to end their studies as he decided to defend the state of Georgia, and he left to join the Confederate army.

The education Susie received was a gift that she wanted to share. Wanting to be of more help to the soldiers than washing their socks, Susie began to help in other ways. She began nursing those who were sick, cooking for the soldiers, and, most importantly, teaching them to read and write. In return, the soldiers taught her how to use a rifle.

Her extra care and love for the soldiers soon came to the attention of the regiment, and she was made daughter of the regiment for the Thirty-Third U.S. Colored Infantry. One solider named Edward King caught Susie's eye, and they were married in 1863.

Susie remained the daughter of the regiment throughout the war and even for a time after. When the Thirty-Third was mustered out, she did not believe her work was done and she set about aiding veterans as well as starting a school for former slaves. Many of the soldiers needed care years later because they still suffered physically or mentally from the war. Many found it hard to adjust to life outside of the military. These men greatly needed the aid that Susie offered. For this she was honored by many veterans long after the war was over.

Called *A Group of Scholars*, this photograph, which was taken in South Carolina during the war, shows some recently freed slave children and young adults with books. (Library of Congress)

A family in a Pennsylvania unit during the war lived in harsh and cramped conditions typical of those who followed the army. (Library of Congress)

Were there any other black women who served as daughters of the regiment?

It is hard to say how many women of African descent served in the capacity of battlefield nurse or daughter of the regiment. Other than Susie Baker, none left memoirs, but there are ways to find out. Some women filed for pensions, or money from the government for their service. These records usually only give a name, but occasionally other interesting information can be found. For example, a Julia Mason is listed as having served as a hospital attendant for the Confederacy. A small note on her pension card even states that she was wounded while in service.[2] Wouldn't it be wonderful to know her story?

Why did so many of the soldiers who had been slaves not know how to read?

Many times, slaves were not allowed to receive an education. It was believed that if a slave was educated, they would then want to be free. Sometimes there were even laws prohibiting slaves from reading. There were others, however, like Susie's master, who believed it was good for everyone to know how to read, whether slave or free. Gen. "Stonewall" Jackson ran a school for slaves so they would know how to read the Bible. Still others, like Pres. Jefferson Davis of the Confederacy, believed in allowing slaves to earn their freedom, and he schooled them so that when they were free, they could make a living.

Susie Baker several decades after the war. (East Carolina University)

Wartime photograph of a soldier in the U.S. Colored Troops with his wife and daughters. (Library of Congress)

Chapter 4

Mary Tepe

Tough Vivandière for the Zouaves

It is a truth that the United States is a country made up of immigrants. In the years preceding the War Between the States, thousands of ships carried individuals fleeing wars or famine in Europe. One country that continually saw turmoil was France. Revolutionaries overturned one form of government after another, and many times it was those who did not have much who suffered the brunt of the abuse.

A fifteen-year-old French girl named Marie Brose was one of these immigrants who crossed the cold Atlantic on a damp sailing vessel in 1849. Her father had just passed away, and looking for more opportunity, her mother packed up and they headed to America, where they settled in Philadelphia.

Not much is known about Mary's childhood other than that she was rather poor and at just sixteen she married a tailor—someone who makes clothes—named Bernardo Tepe (also shown on records as Bernhard Tape).[1] When the war began in 1861, Bernardo **enlisted** with the Twenty-Seventh Pennsylvania **Infantry.** Like most other families at the time, Bernardo expected his wife to take care of the home and his business while he went off to war, but Mary would have none of it. Inspired, no doubt, by the brave and colorful vivandières of her native France, Mary insisted on following her husband into the military.

Since the troops in 1861 were comprised of regiments raised by local governments, there were few set rules governing how the soldiers were to be organized. When Mary showed up, there was most likely doubt as to what to do with a woman, so she was allowed to set up as a **sutler,** selling goods that were not provided as part of the men's regular rations. In addition to selling eggs, vegetables, tobacco, and books, Mary would have undoubtedly taken on other duties of a vivandière, such as nursing, mending, and attempting to boost **morale** while on the march or during battle. However, whether or not she was able to raise the soldiers' spirits is questionable as she was known to be rough and have a surly temper. In fact, despite her popularity during the war, when Frank Moore wrote a book in 1866 compiling the daring and brave women of the Union armies immediately after the war, he omitted Mary as she was not seen as being the best role model for Victorian women—even brave and daring ones.

Despite Mary's flaws, she was courageous and stuck with the Twenty-Seventh Pennsylvania through the first year. Then, in 1862, Bernardo, who was not a good role model for Victorian gentlemen, gambled away the money Mary had earned as a sutler. Furious, Mary left not only her husband but also the Twenty-Seventh. This did not mean the end of the war for her, as she was soon welcomed into the 114th Pennsylvania Infantry, this time as their official vivandière.

The 114th was known as the *Zouaves d'Afrique,* a fancy French name for troops who copied the colorful dress of French Algerian soldiers. Ten years earlier in Europe, there had been a great war called the Crimean War, involving most of the powers in western Europe against Russia. It was an event that Americans had not participated in but followed closely in the papers and read novels and watched plays about. Out of all the troops involved, the French Zouaves became famous for their daring bravery and reputation as tough soldiers. They were the elite soldiers of the Victorian age. Difficult for us in modern times to comprehend, the Zouaves wore bright and very full red trousers. Blue vests and flared jackets trimmed with red cord, bright sashes, white gaiters, leather *jambieres,* which covered the calf muscles, and a tasseled fez with a white turban completed their flamboyant uniforms. As absurd as it may seem in our age when soldiers wear camouflage, the uniforms of the Zouaves brought on awe from those who saw them, and volunteer troops in America were eager to copy the famous French troops. The 114th Pennsylvania wore such a costume and Mary was given a female version of the uniform with a skirt and a wide-brimmed hat with a plume. With her French heritage, she was a perfect fit and the men began to call her "French Mary."

She marched alongside the men on campaign, with a wooden keg full of whiskey on her hip (whiskey was used as medicine for aches, pain, and to calm a wounded soldier) and a heavy Colt .44 revolver on her belt. She slept on the hard ground while on campaign and in a tent when the army settled for a few days. She also followed the soldiers into battle.

At one large battle in December of 1862, in the town of Fredericksburg, Virginia, Mary was working in a field hospital when she was wounded. A large lead **Miníe ball**—a soft, cone-shaped bullet—lodged in her ankle. The surgeons were not able to remove the bullet, and it would cause her pain for the rest of her life.

By the following summer, Mary was recovered enough to return to marching on campaign, and she followed her regiment up into Pennsylvania to a small town called Gettysburg. From July 1 through July 3, 1863, close to 180,000 soldiers fought a battle so horrible that when it was over and the armies left, Americans were left to stare in horror at what had been done. Some 50,000 men lay dead or wounded. Among the casualties was Mary's husband, Bernardo.

Sketch by Alfred R. Waud of a female sutler selling goods from her wagon to members of the Union army. Note how she is armed with a pistol on her belt. (Library of Congress)

Mary stayed behind to bury her husband and help with the difficult task of caring for so many wounded. We do not know how long she stayed in Gettysburg, but we do know that by the next spring, she was again in battle, her skirts riddled with bullets as she ran water to soldiers during the terrible battle at Spotsylvania. Gen. Ulysses S. Grant ordered all women following the Union army to leave, and clearly Mary refused to obey as she was with the 114th Pennsylvania at the end of the war and marched in the grand review in Washington City on May 23, 1865.

After the war, Mary married again and tried to start a new life, but she was always restless. The bullet in her ankle eventually crippled her, and she became terribly poor. It affected her relationship with her husband and she filed for divorce. Eventually, just to survive, she was forced to sell her vivandière uniform. In 1901, she took her own life, a sad end for such a courageous woman.

Mary Tepe in her vivandière uniform, carrying a keg and armed with a revolver. (National Archives)

Why did so many soldiers die during the Civil War?

The War Between the States was devastating for its terribly high number of **casualties.** Advances in weapons had been made, and the conflict saw the wide use of new rifled muskets. Old muskets had smooth barrels and shot a round ball without much accuracy. Rifles have grooves inside the barrel that spins a bullet when it is fired, making it more accurate. (Think of throwing a football versus throwing a soccer ball.) Despite these more accurate weapons, men still fought in tightly formed lines, which was a tactic made successful by Napoleon when muskets were still being used. This horrible combination meant many more men were wounded and killed. Additionally, the .58 caliber **Miníe** bullets were made of soft lead, and when they hit bone, the bones would shatter. If all that was not terrible enough, the relationship between germs and disease would not be understood until after the war, so surgeons and nurses did not know how infection was spread. Oftentimes a surgeon working in a field hospital would not wash his surgical instruments between patients, resulting in many men dying from infection.

Zouave, 1864. Sketch of a Union Zouave by wartime artist Winslow Homer. (National Gallery of Art, Washington, D.C.)

Photograph of Mary Tepe in the field during the aftermath of the battle at Gettysburg. (Special Collections/Musselman Library, Gettysburg College, Gettysburg, Pennsylvania)

A living historian reenacts the firing of an old .58 caliber rifle at the 150th anniversary of the Battle of Pleasant Hill, Louisiana. (Photo by the author)

Chapter 5

Dr. Mary Walker

Medal of Honor Recipient

In the 1850s, when Mary Walker wanted to go to college, there were few options for women who desired to do more than get married and raise a family. Mary wasn't interested in being like other Victorian women; she wanted to be a doctor.

Mary would fight her entire life to have the same rights as men, and it began with her fight to be admitted into Syracuse Medical College. She succeeded and graduated in 1855. Soon afterward, she fell in love with a fellow doctor named Albert Miller, and they were married. Together, they opened their own medical practice. Despite her successes, Mary was difficult to get along with and it wasn't long before Albert decided to break off their partnership and marriage.

It was easy to see that Mary wasn't interested in following the rules society had laid out for her. She refused to wear the corsets or long skirts she was expected to wear and became part of a movement of women in the North who believed in women's suffrage, or equal rights for women, including the right to vote. Many of these suffragettes donned an outfit called the "bloomer dress." It was a radical outfit that included a short, full skirt to the knees and trousers worn beneath.

Many women, such as those who worked in mills or who rode horses while blazing trails in the West, would wear trousers under their dresses while performing hard labor or if it was cold. In some large cities, men and women would exercise or swim in gymnasiums, and there women would wear a similar outfit to the bloomer dress. But for everyday wear out on the street? In public? It was unacceptable. Mary even sometimes took it a few steps further and would skip the short skirt and just wear a coat and trousers. She was heckled for her dress and several times even arrested. Still, she refused to change.

When the war began, there was a dire shortage of doctors and trained nurses. Mary immediately offered to serve as a surgeon, which was a military doctor who held the rank of an officer. The army refused to hire her. They would not even allow her to be a military nurse. Determined, Mary signed on as "contract help" and as a volunteer, which meant she did not have an official position and would not get paid for her work.

Pressing on, Mary insisted on being near the front. She worked in field hospitals, and finally, overburdened with the number of wounded soldiers pouring in from the battlefield at Fredericksburg, Virginia, the army allowed her to perform surgery. Yet when the wounded of Fredericksburg had all been cared for, the army still would not hire her as a surgeon. It took another entire year of tirelessly working in hospitals with no pay before Mary was finally made a surgeon. In September of 1863, around the time of the Battle of Chickamauga, she was made a "Contract Assistant Surgeon," which meant she was a hired civilian surgeon. Nevertheless, she was the first woman surgeon the United States government had hired.[1]

Dr. Mary Walker wearing a "bloomer dress." (Library of Congress)

She was assigned as a surgeon to an Ohio unit but was soon asked if she could serve as a spy. She had previously requested and been turned down by the government for a similar position. This time, however, the answer was yes, and she crossed enemy lines and applied to be a surgeon with the Confederate army. Being a spy was dangerous, as those caught spying were sentenced to death by hanging. Mary was taking a huge risk.

The Confederates were more lenient in allowing women to act as surgeons. They had already hired several female surgeons and had commissioned two women as officers to head military hospitals for the Confederacy. Mary was accepted as an assistant surgeon almost immediately.

She was in a hospital, helping with a surgery in April of 1864, when in the middle of the operation, she was arrested and immediately questioned for being a spy. Not believing Mary's alibi, her captors sent her to a prison in Richmond, Virginia.[2]

Mary sat in prison for four long months. The guards didn't think much of her habit of wearing trousers and offered her dresses to wear, but she refused them. In August, Mary was set free in exchange for a Confederate surgeon who was being held prisoner in the North.

After the war, Mary wanted official recognition for her service so she could apply for the benefits bestowed upon veterans. Her request was partially granted. She would receive a pension due to health issues that arose from her time in prison, but she still would not be an official member of the U.S. Military.

In November of 1865, Pres. Andrew Johnson decided to bestow upon Mary the Congressional Medal of Honor. To date, Mary Walker is the only woman to have received the highest award given by the U.S. Military. Sadly, in 1916 the military felt too many Medals of Honor had been given and rescinded those that did not fit certain criteria. One of those criteria was that the recipient had to have been in actual combat with the enemy, so the military asked Mary to give her medal back! Mary, who wore the medal daily on her suit of clothes, refused. She continued to wear the medal until her death in 1919, even though officially the honor had been revoked.

Nearly sixty years after her death, upon hearing the story of Mary Walker, a military board reinstated Mary's honor in 1977.

Dr. Mary Walker post-war wearing trousers and her Medal of Honor. (National Library of Medicine)

A military hospital in Fredericksburg, Virginia, toward the end of the war. Note the woman seated in the doorway. She is most likely a visitor or volunteer nurse. (Library of Congress)

Chapter 6

Bridget Divers

Joined the Cavalry

Tracking down the real Bridget Divers is a difficult task. Shortly after the war, books and newspapers recorded her heroism, and Frank Moore featured Bridget in his first chapter. But actual records for Bridget are hard to find. Even the spelling of her name is difficult to know for certain. This may be because she never learned to read or write and signed her name with a simple X.

What we do know is that Bridget was born in Ireland around 1835 and immigrated to America when she was about ten years old. In 1861, she went to war with her husband. Only one soldier with a name close to Divers is recorded in the rolls of the First Michigan Volunteer Cavalry Regiment, the regiment that claims her service time and again. His name was William Devere, and he volunteered in August of 1861. In November of 1862, he is listed as **deserted.**[1] However, there were many times a soldier was listed as having run away before the army found out he had been killed or taken prisoner. There are accounts that William was wounded on the field in 1862. It is possible that he died later from his wounds. Yet other accounts tell of Bridget heading west after the war with her husband. Ultimately, whether she worked entirely alone like Annie Etheridge and Mary Tepe or had a husband near her side is unknown.

The First Michigan **Cavalry** was led by Gen. George Armstrong Custer, the same General Custer who would be killed by the Sioux at the Battle of the Little Bighorn in 1876. His cavalry wore red flowing scarves and called themselves "The Wolverines." Bridget would gallop upon her horse beside them, the saddlebags in her kit filled with medicine, bandages, and items such as books or needles and thread to help ease the lives of the soldiers in camp. She wore a simple dress with trousers beneath her skirt and a soldier's cap upon her head. Some say she added a feminine touch by securing it with a hat pin. Her Irish upbringing and heritage were obvious as she spoke with a rough brogue and had bright red hair. The men called her "Irish Biddy" with fondness as she cared for them in camp and on the battlefield.

Most of a soldier's service was spent in camp, waiting to march and fight. During these times, Bridget would help with laundry, mending, and cooking and would often work with the Christian Commission, which was an organization that tended to the needs of soldiers on both sides. Bridget would work to bring supplies, including Bibles and religious tracts, to the soldiers in General Custer's brigade. She was often accompanied by other women on her errands.[2]

It is the women with whom she worked in field hospitals and the Christian Commission who wrote down accounts of meeting her and visiting with Bridget who give us what information we know. One such woman was a nurse named Charlotte McKay, who wrote in her 1876 memoir:

> She has been with the cavalry all the time, going out with them on their cavalry raids—always ready to succor the wounded on the field—often getting men off who, but for her, would be left to die, and, fearless of shell or bullet, among the last to leave. Protected by officers and respected by privates, with her little sunburnt face, she makes her home in the saddle or the shelter-tent; often, indeed sleeping in the open air without a tent.[3]

Another woman, Mary Livermore with the U.S. Sanitary Commission, wrote in 1888:

> Sometimes when a soldier fell she took his place, fighting in his stead with unquailing courage. Sometimes she rallied retreating troops—sometimes she brought off the wounded from the field—always fearless and daring, always doing good service as a soldier.[4]

This last account tells how Bridget went to battle. She was not content to sit behind with the supply wagons nor in a hospital tent and had several horses shot out from under her. One was even stolen while her unit slept near the Confederates led by General John S. Mosby.[5] While tending to the wounded was her priority, she sometimes picked up a rifle and fought back. Her plain skirts had holes from bullets that whistled close.

After the war, Bridget disappeared. No record can be found of where she went, though some say she followed her husband out west. Perhaps she followed General Custer, but there is no evidence and we can only guess.

The Christian Commission at Gettysburg in August 1863. There were two main civilian organizations created during the war to aid soldiers: the Christian Commission and the Sanitary Commission. While the Sanitary Commission was secular, the Christian Commission also saw after the soldiers' spiritual health. Members made an oath to help anyone who needed it and there were several times when they got into trouble for treating Confederate soldiers the same as Union soldiers. Vivandières worked closely with both organizations to be sure aid came to the soldiers they tended. (Library of Congress)

A group of living historians portrays Union cavalry at a battle reenactment. Bridget would have had a horse and would have ridden alongside the men while on the march. She also rode her horse into battle so she could tend to the wounded. (Photo by the author)

A romanticized lithograph of Bridget in battle. (A.D. Worthington & Co. Publishers, 1887)

What did women like Bridget take with them to war?

Some women who followed the soldiers to war would wear feminine versions of the soldiers' uniforms while others would wear riding habits or a plain dress. Working women of the time would often wear pants under their skirts and they would, of course, not wear the cumbersome petticoats or hoops! She would also be sure to have a hat to protect her face from the sun, a bag with food, and a few personal items as well as a Bible, medicine, and religious tracts. Commonly, she would be armed with some sort of revolver and many would carry a keg that was filled with wine, water, or whiskey, which was helpful for a wounded soldier in pain.

A reproduction Union vivandière uniform modeled after early war examples with sash, belt, side-lacing women's shoes, haversack for carrying food, and keg. Many times the skirts worn by women who took to the battlefield had bold stripes along the hem. Presumably the stripe, easy to spot across the battlefield, would have alerted enemy soldiers that the wearer was a woman. (Photo by the author)

The Confederate spy Belle Boyd after the war, wearing a military-inspired costume with a Confederate military jacket. (Berkeley County Historical Society, West Virginia)

Part 2

Women for the Gray

FIGHTING FOR SOUTHERN INDEPENDENCE

Chapter 7

Capt. Sally Tompkins

The Angel of the Confederacy

Like any other girl growing up in Virginia during the 1830s and '40s, Sally Tompkins wore pretty dresses, went to school and church, and learned to sew and cook. Most importantly, she was taught how to care for people who were injured or sick. First aid skills were important for women to learn so that they could treat family members. Doctors were rarely consulted and then only if someone was very sick. Most of the time, it was up to the mother or a sister to nurse a member of the household back to health.

In 1842, when Sally was nine years old, a doctor was called to her home. Much of her family had become very ill and she lost three of her sisters. From then on, Sally worked hard to help others who were unwell. She would offer her nursing skills to anyone who needed assistance, whether they were free or a slave.

When Virginia joined the Confederate States of America in 1861, war soon followed. Wars gather together many soldiers who must live and work in a small area. The Civil War was no different. As a result, sickness bred in the camps. After battles, there were also thousands of wounded. Pres. Jefferson Davis called for volunteers to help in hospitals as nurses. This, of course, was exactly what Sally was good at.

Sally visited a judge who had a large house in Richmond, the capital of the Confederacy, and asked if he would be willing to lend his house for a hospital. The judge agreed. Next Sally sought volunteers to work in her hospital. Many women rushed to help. Rich and poor, slave and free, soon all were taking orders from Sally, who insisted on a spotlessly clean hospital.[1]

Doctors in the 1860s did not know about germs yet, so cleanliness was not thought to be important. However, it was extremely important to Sally, and Sally's patients were known for getting better. The patients in her hospital did so well, in fact, that when President Davis ordered that all hospitals had to have a military officer in charge, he decided not to replace Sally. Instead, he made her an officer. Sally became a captain![2] "Captain Sally," as the men called her, saved more than a thousand lives during the war. She did her best, comforting and tending to each soldier who was brought to the hospital.

During most of the war, the Union blocked much-needed supplies from coming into the Confederacy. This included medicine. Sally used her family's money to pay men with fast ships to try and outrace the Union warships so she could get medicine for her hospital. Sadly, there were times when she had to make do and keep her hospital running despite lacking necessary supplies.

In April of 1865, Richmond had to be abandoned and much of it burned as Northern soldiers took control of the capital. As flames consumed the city, Sally refused to leave the soldiers. The hospital was spared from burning and when the Union army came, brave Sally made sure her patients continued to receive good care.

Capt. Sally Tompkins around the time of the war. (American Civil War Museum)

How did the North prevent supplies from reaching the South?

The Union set up a barricade called a **blockade** around the South during the war. The blockade stopped all goods, including much-needed food, medicine, and even Bibles, from entering or leaving Confederate states. So how did any medicine get through the blockade? Some goods came in on fast ships that could race past the Union warships. Other goods were smuggled in on people. Medicine was sometimes hidden in dolls or toys and concealed under women's skirts when they crossed the border from North to South. Women who were caught were usually thrown into prison.

The ruins of burned buildings after the fall of Richmond in April 1865. Sally would have seen the city burn around her. (Library of Congress)

In this illustration, a Southern woman who was stopped by the Union military is searched for items banned from entering the South. She has hidden quinine—medicine used to bring down fevers—in the bustle pad that goes under her dress. (*Harper's Weekly*, 1863, accessed via the American Civil War Museum)

Chapter 8

Nancy Hart

Teenaged Spy and Scout

Nancy Hart grew up with brothers who taught her to ride horses and shoot rifles. She loved these activities, and they fed her adventurous spirit, which sometimes led her far from home. When she became a teenager, she chose to live with her sister Mary in the woods of present-day West Virginia. This became a problem in 1861 as Nancy's parents and brothers decided to support the Union while Nancy's sister supported the new Confederacy. What side would Nancy choose?

Even though her family was anti-slavery, at first Nancy seemed unsure as to whether she would support the Union or the Confederacy. One family account tells how Nancy and her father witnessed a slave being whipped and that they were disturbed by the "shameful" event.[1] However, the issues that led Virginia to join the Confederacy were not limited to slavery. For most people like Nancy—and a handsome young man named Joshua Douglas, who joined a band of Confederate raiders called the Moccasin Rangers[2]—slavery was of little concern to them or their personal way of life.

Aside from the young raider who had Nancy's eye, Nancy's sister Mary was married to a supporter of the Confederacy named William Price. One day, William decided to help some Confederate soldiers who were on a scouting mission. When the Union soldiers found out, they murdered William. Mary was heartbroken and Nancy was furious. From that moment on, Nancy decided that she was going to fight for the South.

As a girl of fifteen, she wasn't allowed to be a soldier, but Nancy knew the land and offered to work as a spy for the Confederacy. She would look for Union soldiers, listen to them talk, and then race her pony to a Confederate officer and tell him what she had heard. Soon the Union soldiers found out about her and put out a reward for her arrest.

Despite the danger, Nancy continued to gather information and spy on Union troops. It was not long before she was caught. In July of 1862, she was captured while out riding. A blue-coated officer named Colonel Starr held Nancy prisoner in a house while he decided what to do with her.

By that time, Nancy had become famous. Her name had been in the news in both the North and the South. Colonel Starr, feeling very proud to have caught her, made her wear a pretty dress and have her picture made so he could sell it to the newspapers. Nancy didn't want her picture made so she just looked angrily at the camera and refused to smile. She swore that she would escape.[3]

That night, Nancy managed to trick a guard. She stole his gun and then stole the colonel's horse. She galloped away and rode hard until she found a Confederate officer. She explained the details of her capture but also provided him information about what the Union troops were up to. After hearing all that Nancy had to say, the Confederates planned an attack on Colonel Starr. A week later, they managed to capture him and his men.

Nancy then became even more famous, but we do not know of any further exploits after she escaped Colonel Starr. She did marry the handsome ranger, Joshua Douglas, and remained with him until her death in 1912. Her story continued to be told as far away as London, and songs calling her a hero were written. So many stories have been told that it has become difficult to know truth from legend. Whatever the truth may be, we know that her amazing deeds have kept people talking and writing about her for more than a century and a half.

This photograph is believed to be the photo taken of Nancy the night she was captured. (*Photographic History of the Civil War, Volume 8*)

A Union scout makes his way through the backwoods of Louisiana. Scouts were an integral part of both armies. Scouts could be soldiers or individuals who volunteered from local communities. Their job was to be the "eyes and ears" of an army, discovering the best places for the army to march and keeping track of the enemy's movements. While most scouts were men, there are several accounts of women who performed scouting duties. (Library of Congress)

Belle Boyd after the war. She wrote a book about her exploits and traveled all over the country acting out different scenes from her experiences as a spy. (National Archives)

What was it like to be a female spy?

Many women served their respective countries as spies during the war. There was danger in being a spy as the penalty if caught was death. However, the sensibilities of the era frowned on executing women, so women who were captured were often thrown into prison. Spies came from all strata of society. In one case, Mary Elizabeth Bowser, a black schoolteacher from Philadelphia, risked her life posing as a free woman and was hired on as a servant in the household of Pres. Jefferson Davis. Other women became spies out of chance as the war had come to their doorsteps and they wanted to find a way to help. Such women included Mary Kate Patterson of Tennessee, who captured a Union spy in her own dining room, and Belle Boyd, who began spying at the age of seventeen when Union soldiers invaded her home and took over her town. Belle was eventually caught and held in Old Capitol Prison in Washington, D.C.

Chapter 9

Mary Sophia Hill

Irish National, Southern Heroine

History is complicated and the reasons behind war are complex. What made so many men and women sacrifice their comfort, safety, livelihoods, and even lives beginning in 1861? Only by reading individual letters, diaries, and memoirs can we begin to grasp what spurred the people of the past—who had different beliefs and a different culture from our own—to go to war.

If we look at the politics—what the governments of the states were doing—war was motivated by the major issues of slavery, unfair taxes for the Southern states, and vast cultural differences between the North and the South that can be traced all the way back to the founding of Jamestown and the Pilgrims at Plymouth. These political reasons ignited a powder keg in April of 1861.

Ultimately, most individuals had their own reasons for supporting one side or the other. Many of those who supported the Union believed in the American republic, which was only eighty years old, and wanted to see it succeed. They feared that if the country was divided, it would spell doom for the new and great nation created by the Founding Fathers such as Thomas Jefferson, James Madison, and Alexander Hamilton. Southerners, on the other hand, felt abused by the government in Washington but held a fierce loyalty to their home state. They believed the federal government had abandoned the ideas of Jefferson and Madison and become a new Britain that they needed to free themselves from. They were re-creating the fight of their grandparents. In their mind's eye, they were fighting a second American Revolution.

Many other reasons abounded for each man and each woman caught up in the conflict. One woman who had a different reason for leaving the comforts of home and suffering through the hardships of army life was Mary Sophia Hill.

Mary was not even an American; she was Irish. Unlike other Irish women included in this book such as Bridget Divers, Mary considered herself a **subject** of the United Kingdom, which ruled Ireland at the time. She often traveled back and forth across the Atlantic to visit family in Ireland. Mary was also different from many

A woman named Florence Nightingale became famous for tending to the wounded during the Crimean War (1853-1856). Since European immigrants to America brought with them memories of that war, many women volunteered to help in the War Between the States in hopes of becoming an "American Florence Nightingale." Pictured is a woman dispensing food and drink to French and British soldiers in Crimea. (Photo by Roger Fenton, Library of Congress)

women who chose to follow the army on the march and into the field of battle in another way: Mary was highly educated. When she had arrived in New Orleans ten years earlier, she quickly found jobs as a teacher of French and a music instructor.[1]

In 1861, she was forty-two years old and had never been married, but she was not alone. She had a younger brother named Samuel with whom she lived in Louisiana. In her diary, Mary admits she never had any intention of getting involved with the war and had even suggested to Sam that they go back to Ireland until all the trouble blew over. Sam disagreed. The brother and sister had a horrible fight, and in the end, Sam walked out in a huff. Not wanting to return to the house with his sister, he enlisted in the Sixth Louisiana Infantry.

There are two sides to every argument, and after a big fight, those involved usually feel some regret for things they said or did. Mary felt this way. In fact, she felt awful. Samuel didn't have to join the army—he wasn't a **citizen** of Louisiana; he was a British subject!—and his life was now in danger. Mary decided it was now her duty to do what she could to see that her brother survived the war. She packed a few items and attached herself to the Sixth Louisiana **Infantry** as a laundress and nurse.

She first traveled to the busy city of Richmond, Virginia, which had become the new capital of the Confederacy. It was teeming with soldiers, merchants, politicians, and doctors. Mary was able to set herself up as a nurse, and when the battles began to rage, she traveled with the surgeons and helped with the wounded who came to the field hospitals.

Mary had her work cut out for her. Not only did she deal with the hardships of bumping along in a wagon over dusty or muddy roads, sleeping in a tent, and eating the meager rations soldiers ate, but her main reason for joining in the first place, to take care of her brother Sam, was not an easy task. Sam was not a good soldier. He was often sick and he had a propensity for losing things. He would lose his jacket or his bayonet. He'd lose some of his leather **accoutrements** such as his **cartridge box,** and poor Mary would scramble and scrounge to replace them before he got into trouble for having lost them.

During one horrible **campaign,** Mary received news that Sam had been killed on the battlefield. She was sick with worry and dashed to the battlefield to find him. Luckily, he was alive, though wounded. For weeks she stayed in the city of Charlottesville tending to her brother as well as to many more wounded and sick soldiers. She wrote the names of the soldiers she tended in her diary and some of them, despite everything she did, still died.

She also wrote of the difficulties of working in a field hospital.

There were few comforts and the doctors were short on almost every needed supply. At one point, Mary was pulling down curtains from houses to make bandages. She weathered terrible storms where she spent the entire night awake, soaking wet, straining on ropes and hammering at stakes to keep the great big hospital tents from falling down. Several times she was told the enemy was drawing near and she would be in danger if she stayed. She stayed anyway.

In the middle of the war, in 1863, she used her status as a British subject to travel to Ireland. While there, she spoke to the many people overseas who supported the Confederacy. Some had sons who had left to fight in the Southern states and she told them what news she could. She returned to Louisiana laden with gifts of supplies from the people in Ireland.

Her trip made her realize how much the families of the soldiers wanted news of how their sons or husbands were faring. There were many times when a loved one was ill or wounded and if the family had known sooner, they could have traveled to him and administered help or been with him as he died. One of the problems faced by family members was that when the Union army invaded an area, they did not allow any letters to be sent in or out. Mary decided to take upon the dangerous task of smuggling letters through enemy lines, hoping her status as a foreigner would keep her safe.

She helped hundreds of families keep in contact with their loved ones on the battlefield and soldiers communicate with those at home. For her previous work as a nurse on the battlefields of Virginia and then as a daring messenger, she became well known among those in the South. Unfortunately, her deeds did not go unnoticed by the enemy, and in 1864 she was caught with a letter from none other than her brother Sam and was arrested.

Union authorities accused her of **espionage.** They said she was a spy. The penalty for spies was death! Mary pleaded with her captors and reminded them that she was a British subject, but they did not care. She was thrown into a cold prison cell where she became sick. She was held for four long months until she became so ill that her captors worried she might die and set her free.

Mary never fully recovered and suffered weakness and pain in her joints from her imprisonment for the rest of her life. Despite this, she decided she was not done helping the soldiers from Louisiana. After the war was over, she set up the first soldiers' home for ailing or impoverished soldiers. When she died in 1901, the soldiers showed how much they appreciated what she had done and a huge procession of gray-clad veterans marched through the streets of New Orleans. They draped her coffin in a Confederate flag and gave her all the military honors of an officer as they laid her to rest in Greenwood Cemetery.

During Mary's time, there were no televisions, no radios, no computers, and no phones. The telegraph was relatively new and telegrams were reserved mainly for official and government business. The only way for the soldiers to keep in touch with loved ones at home was through letters and by reading newspapers that were brought into camps. Letter writing was very important and soldiers were thirsty for the written word, reading everything they could get their hands on. Smuggling letters, books, Bibles, and newspapers across the lines became a very important job for a number of Southern women. (*News from Home*, 1863, by Edwin Forbes, Library of Congress)

A woman tending to the wounded on the field the night after a battle. (*Midnight on the Battlefield, 1887*, A.D. Worthington & Co. Publishers)

Union field hospital at Savage Station, Virginia. Mary would have seen a similar scene while helping in Confederate field hospitals. (Library of Congress)

Chapter 10

Sindy Riller Boles

Wild Texas Cinderella

The story of Sindy Riller "Cinderella" Boles begins as a tale of true love out of the Old West. Sindy grew up on the banks of the Trinity River in a town called Trinidad, Texas. She was a tomboy. She rode horses, was known to be good with a rifle, and often wore trousers. Her father died when she was only eleven, and Sindy grew to be even more independent.

According to family lore, one day when Sindy was fifteen years old, she was off riding her horse and came home to find a new boarder at her house. He was a dapper Yankee from Massachusetts, fresh out of law school. The Yankee lawyer was named Ben Swearingen, and bored at the idea of settling down to practice law in Boston, he had decided to take a vacation and see the "wilds" of Texas for himself. He even hoped to catch a glimpse of the aging Texas hero Sam Houston, who was a friend of the Boles family and the reason Ben had been drawn to find boarding at their home.

The story continues that while Ben was sitting on the front porch trying to catch a cool breeze on a hot summer day, Sindy rode up on her horse. She was dusty and wearing trousers, and as she dismounted and ascended the porch steps, she began to swear about the Texas heat. Rather than be put off by this unladylike display, Ben was intrigued, even beguiled, by Sindy's flushed face and rough demeanor.

Whether the family story is true, what is known for a fact is that the Massachusetts lawyer married Sindy and they soon had a son.

Ben became less dapper and buckled down to the harder life found in Texas.

When war was declared in 1861 and Texas voted to secede and join the new Confederacy, Ben's loyalties were with his new homeland and he joined one of the roughest Texas units, the Twelfth Texas Cavalry, a unit called Parson's Dragoons. Sindy, like the rest of the women in town, sorrowfully watched her husband ride off on his horse, not knowing if she would ever see him again.

She did not.

Ben died of camp fever (usually typhoid), two years later, in 1863, when the unit was stationed near Hot Springs, Arkansas. When news reached Sindy, she was heartbroken. She became restless and began to wonder if she had been there to tend her husband, if she had gone like some women did to nurse the sick, whether Ben would have lived. Soon she also learned that one reason so many of the soldiers had died that season was because the **blockade**—the Union blocking of goods from entering the South—of food and medicine had prevented the soldiers from receiving the goods they desperately needed.

That settled it. Sindy went to the county leaders and requested permission to leave with a wagon full of supplies to help the soldiers. Hesitant at first, local leaders knew there was no quelling the strong will of Sindy, and they consented. In fact, they paid her thirty-eight dollars to make her nearly three-hundred-mile run. But Sindy didn't care about the money. She left her son with a sister and headed out for Arkansas.[1]

For two years, Sindy made runs, sometimes through enemy lines, to bring bandages, medicine, clothes, and other comforts to the soldiers at the front.

Sindy in 1868. (Private collection)

A former slave named Ely Irvine, who had fought in the Texas Revolution, rode shotgun on Sindy's journeys into Arkansas and Louisiana. The men began to await her arrival, and once amongst the gray lines, she'd sometimes stay for a time and nurse the sick. The men gave her the nickname Cinderella, which she'd carry with her for the rest of her life.

Running wagons through enemy lines was dangerous business. Some living historians in Texas reenact the capture of a Confederate wagon by Union cavalry. (Photo by the author)

Chapter 11

Lucy Ann Cox

Honored Tagalong

Lucy Ann White was the daughter of a newspaper editor in Fredericksburg, Virginia. Most local papers at the time were small, run out of a tiny office that included a hand-crank printing press and drawers full of letters that had to be individually laid. Just before the war was an especially busy time for newspapers. With the political turmoil and Virginia's decision to **secede** from the United States and join the Confederacy, Lucy's father undoubtedly had a lot of news to print. He needed extra help so he hired a young man named James Cox as his **apprentice** and aide. When James began working in the small printing office, Lucy fell in love.[1]

On April 12, 1861, the first shots of the war were fired in South Carolina at a place called Fort Sumter. Pres. Abraham Lincoln then called for 75,000 troops to invade the South. Citizens of Virginia quickly formed units of volunteers to defend their homeland against the Northerners. In Fredericksburg, the Thirtieth Virginia Infantry was raised, and James joined as a soldier. When the Thirtieth Virginia moved out and headed north to meet the invading army, Lucy decided to drop everything and follow.

She tagged along behind James' regiment all the way to the first major battle of the war at Manassas, Virginia. The Thirtieth Virginia arrived at Manassas Junction the day of the battle but was too late to participate. However, Lucy did not miss the opportunity to help the wounded, and afterward she did not go home but stayed near the army, helping where she could. That November, James was struck with **rheumatism,** a common ailment among the soldiers at the time. Lucy stayed near his bedside. In January of 1862, James and Lucy got married. Now she was Mrs. Lucy Ann Cox.

The spring was harsh, and Lucy followed James closely, administering to him and the rest of his company. When they were not marching, she was mending and washing, cooking, and tending to the ill. When in battle, she carried canteens and bandages. She tended to wounds before a wounded soldier could get to the field hospital. Bullets nipped at her skirts, but she pressed on.[2] She witnessed the battles around Richmond such as those called the Seven Days Battles. She marched northward, waded across the Potomac River into Maryland, and suffered through the bloodiest day of the war at Sharpsburg on September 17, 1862.

After the Battle of Sharpsburg, it was a sad trek back to Virginia.

Southerners often had to take cover from exploding artillery shells when their cities were under siege by the Union army. This lithograph created several years after the war shows a shell exploding in a Union field hospital. It was very rare for hospitals to be targeted. (*A Rebel Shell Bursting in a Union Hospital*, 1887, A.D. Worthington & Co. Publishers)

The battle had not gone well. The army, now under Gen. Robert E. Lee, had hoped that by heading north they could end the war, but it was not meant to be.

Three months later, on December 11, the armies met in Lucy's hometown of Fredericksburg. Many of the battles so far had been fought in farmers' fields, but Fredericksburg was different. A river flowed through the town, and the Confederate army did not want the Union army to cross it. Confederate **sharpshooters,** soldiers who are extremely good shots, hid themselves in homes along the riverbank and shot at any enemy soldiers who tried to cross the river. To counter the Confederates' defense, the Union brought **artillery**—large cannon—and began to shell the town. Iron shells filled with gunpowder exploded over homes, businesses, and churches. Houses were blown apart and caught fire. Lucy watched as her hometown—her home and her father's printing shop where she met James—was targeted by exploding bombs.

The Union soldiers eventually made it across the river. There were so many of them that the Confederate efforts could not stop them. The Thirtieth Virginia, along with the rest of General Lee's army, retreated to a hill called Marye's Heights outside of town. Many Union soldiers died trying to take that hill. It was a horrible day and night, and there were wounded to tend to for weeks afterward. Lucy spent Christmas around Fredericksburg tending to the sick and wounded.

James became sick the next year, and Lucy followed him home. Sometimes he had to stay in a hospital in Richmond. He and Lucy did not miss many battles while James recovered because the Thirtieth Virginia fought very little until the spring of 1864. By that time, Gen. Ulysses S. Grant had taken over the Union army in Virginia and he fought harder than any of the Union generals before him. Times became grim for the Confederates and the Thirtieth Virginia. At a place called Cold Harbor, in June of 1864, James was shot in the hand.

Lucy accompanied James to a large hospital in Richmond called Chimborazo. There he had to have part of his right hand **amputated.** After recovering, James decided to return to his regiment but found it difficult to be a soldier without his right thumb. In February of 1865, he decided to go home and Lucy followed him.[3]

After the war, many of the veterans whom Lucy had helped wanted to see her again. They held reunions and invited Lucy to attend. Even though she had never been an official part of the Confederate army, just a caring tagalong who had done what she could to help, the veterans made her an official member of their veterans' organizations and even erected a monument in her name.

What might Lucy and other Confederate daughters of the regiment have worn? It is hard to know exactly what an individual woman would have worn as there are few descriptions and even fewer photographs. Some may have dressed as fancy vivandières early in the war, but those outfits would have quickly deteriorated under the harsh conditions of army life. A pretty bodice might have been replaced with an extra shirt from one of the soldiers and a cast-off jacket. Soft ladies' boots would have been destroyed by the first hard march and substituted with something from the commissary if necessary. Whatever they wore, it would have been sensible and of material easy to procure. (Reproduction Confederate vivandière kit in the author's collection)

Confederate veterans meet in 1921 at the Confederate Reunion Grounds in Mexia, Texas. Note one woman, far bottom right, was invited to have her photo taken with the veterans. (Private collection)

How did veterans remember the war?

Soldiers who have seen the hardships of war suffer from both physical and mental wounds. Civil War veterans often had injuries that still hurt or terrible nightmares about the battles they had seen. Many of the women who served the soldiers during the war served them after they returned home. They worked to establish soldiers' homes for the ill or poor veterans and also aided in the organization of reunions.

In the North, Union veterans started an organization called the Grand Army of the Republic (GAR), and members would host reunions where the veterans could gather and support each other. They raised monuments to the dead and money to help widows and orphans.

In the South, it was a little harder for the former soldiers to gather together for support as many of the Confederate veterans returned to destroyed homes and crops. They were also **disenfranchised,** which means they could not vote. The government in Washington, D.C. broke the South up into five military districts ruled by the army. Former Confederate soldiers were not allowed to gather in any large number for twelve years during a period called **Reconstruction.** After Reconstruction, during the 1880s, Confederate veterans finally began to hold reunions similar to their GAR counterparts.

Women who had accompanied the armies as nurses or vivandières were known to attend reunions and the dedication of monuments in both the North and South.

Chapter 12

Oriana Moon

Surgeon at Manassas

Oriana, or "Orie" as her family called her, was taught that she should pursue her dreams. In the nineteenth century, women often found their options limited, as most colleges were for men only and many jobs excluded women. Women could not even vote. Orie's father disagreed with the rules society placed on women. When Orie was young, her father bought her a library because she loved to read and he offered to send her to school wherever she wanted to go. He promised the same to Orie's four sisters. Her older sister wanted to be a teacher. Her younger sisters, Lottie and Edmonia, didn't know what they wanted to be yet, but Orie knew. She wanted to be a doctor.

She left her home near Charlottesville, Virginia, to go to the Female Medical College of Pennsylvania in Philadelphia. While there, she focused on the workings of the heart as well as general health. As forward thinking as the college was, believing in women who wanted to become doctors, the rest of society was not so open to the idea. Knowing this, when Orie returned home, she did not open a medical practice. Instead, she tended to local women and slave families. Since her family was rather wealthy and could support her, she felt her work was one way she could give back to her community.

She had not been practicing medicine long when an adventurous opportunity became available to her. An uncle invited her to go on a mission trip to Jerusalem and Egypt. Not only would she be able to see the ancient Holy Land, but she also might be able to explore medical practices overseas and help those to whom her uncle was going to be ministering.

They embarked on a long voyage on a clipper ship then traveled by horse, carriage, and boat. Although Orie was a genteel Southern lady, her father had also taught her how to shoot, and she carried a revolver on her person—and twice had to pull it.

Once in Jerusalem, she visited the holy landmarks and began helping her uncle with his mission work among the nomadic Bedouin tribes. He would share his Christian faith while Orie saw to those who needed medical help, especially children. It was a hot, dusty, and strange place for her, but she found enjoyment in helping others. When she returned to Virginia, she had not only fantastic stories to tell but also greater medical experience.

When war came to Virginia in July of 1861, the entire Moon family pitched in to help. They gave money and supplies, and Orie wrote a polite letter offering her services as a doctor to the Confederate army. In her letter, she wrote, "Please say to the authorities, that I will give the services of myself and servant gratuitously, if they are willing to incur our expenses for dwelling and board. I will go anywhere or do anything they may see fit to assign me, if it is to follow the army and seek the wounded on the field of battle."[1] In her letter she mentions a servant, so she may have had a slave acting as an assistant to her.

At first she received no reply. Her younger sister Lottie, who was better with words, tried writing and still there was no reply. It wasn't until wounded began pouring in from the first battle at Manassas that her ability to help was recognized. The university in Charlottesville was converted into a great hospital and when it overflowed with patients, local homes were offered up to house the wounded. When Orie came in person to offer her help, she was not only accepted, she was also made a surgeon and put in charge of an entire ward!

Orie toiled day and night performing surgeries and evaluating patients. She only rested for short periods. During this time, she was pulled from her work to see to a patient another doctor did not know how to help. A young soldier had been wounded in the hand but lay on the hospital bed extremely ill. By the soldier's bedside was another soldier standing worriedly over him. Orie found out the young soldier at the bedside was the patient's brother, John Andrews.

John and his brother Robert had just come from the battlefield. They had joined the army together, along with a third brother, Billie, in their home state of Alabama. Billie was already dead. He had been killed in the battle and hastily buried in an unmarked grave. John was beside himself, worried he was going to lose his remaining brother. Coincidentally, he was a doctor, and he and Orie spent several days trying to save Robert's life. Sadly, they did not succeed. John had little money and was heartbroken that he would have to bury Robert in the same manner as Billie. Orie decided to help, and she paid for John to accompany his brother's body home by train.

Orie continued to work in the hospital, and some time later she was surprised when John returned, this time offering his help as a doctor rather than as a soldier. He must have had hopes of working alongside Orie, but Orie soon became ill herself and had to return home. John decided to repay her kindness and after working in the hospital by day, he would go to the Moons' home in the evenings and tend to Orie. A fondness deepened between the two and in December, John and Orie were married.

Hastily dug graves on the Manassas battlefield. (Library of Congress)

Orie's health never truly recovered and the following year she had a child, so she was not able to return to her position as surgeon. John tried to find work as a field surgeon but was unsuccessful, so he returned to administer to those on the home front.

The war raged on, and at one point the Moon home was ransacked by Union troops. Luckily, a slave of the family courageously drove a wagon laden with food into hiding, saving the family from starvation.

If Oriana and John thought the end of the war would be the end of their troubles, they were sadly mistaken. The South was scorched and destitute. John practiced medicine but his patients had neither money to pay nor much to **barter.** He decided to pack up the family and move to Alabama, hoping things there were better. They were not.

Although Orie had grown up in a grand house surrounded by her books, she and John now lived in a two-room shack. Despite the rough new life, Orie remained hopeful and was known for her kindness. The family moved again, this time to Tennessee, where they hoped to find patients who could pay and offer their growing family—they had several children now—a more comfortable life where hunger was not always at their door. But poverty was everywhere in the South.

While John worked long hours, travelling to patients all over the hills of Tennessee, Orie organized a Bible school for local friends and invited former slaves and women to come as well. Around this time, her sister Lottie came to visit. Lottie was so inspired when she saw the many people coming to Orie's Bible school, set up beneath a tree, that she decided to go into mission work like their uncle had before the war. Lottie would go on to become a missionary in China with her sister Edmonia.

Not everyone was impressed with Orie's work after the war. In addition to the day-to-day struggle just to rebuild and find enough to eat, there were **carpetbaggers,** men and women who came from the North to exploit the South, who were driving up taxes and forcing some poor Southerners off their land. Sometimes they would lease the land to former slaves. This created a lot of anger and resentment, and some Southerners took out their frustrations with violence. They attacked and intimidated the carpetbaggers and the former slaves. Groups such as the Ku Klux Klan organized these attacks. When some members of a local Klan saw the many people gathering at Orie and John's home—including many former slaves—they thought Orie was stirring up the former slaves to cause trouble. Since Orie and John were not from Tennessee, the Klan also thought they might be carpetbaggers.

One day while John was away on call, a group of Klan members decided to attack Orie. Fortunately, some locals learned of the plan and warned Orie. They managed to head off the Klan and convince them that Orie was only teaching the Bible and that she was not a Yankee carpetbagger. Still, the episode frightened the family, and John and Orie decided to move back to Virginia.[2]

Orie lived the last years of her life in Virginia. She had never truly recovered her health after serving as a surgeon during the war, and childbirth made her weaker. She had her last child, a son, when she was forty-six years old and passed away three years later. Though she died before turning fifty, she led a full and amazing life. Most importantly, she did good for many people in many places.

John and Oriana. (Courtesy of Woman's Missionary Union, SBC)

Chapter 13

Betsy Sullivan

Vivandière and POW

The people of Tennessee voted to join the Confederate States of America on June 8, 1861. It was the last state to do so, but many of its young men were already members of local **militias,** which became regiments in the fight for their new nation. In Pulaski, the young men joined a regiment called the First Tennessee Infantry. Among their ranks was a man named John Sullivan.

John had a wife named Betsy, an Irish woman who had immigrated to America and made Tennessee her home. They had been married for some time but had no children. Not wanting to be left alone at home, Betsy decided she would follow her husband and not only offer him aid whenever needed, but also be a "mother" to all the young men in the regiment. Soon after they set out, the soldiers began to call her "Mother Sullivan."

While some women who followed the armies, such as most nurses and laundresses, rode in wagons with the supplies, Betsy stayed close to her husband, carrying her items on her back and marching alongside the soldiers. As one member of the regiment described, "She marched on foot with her knapsack on her back through the mountains of West Virginia, slept on the frozen ground, under the cold skies, a blanket her only covering—her knapsack, her pillow."[1]

The First Tennessee was assigned to one of the hardest marching brigades, the one under Gen. Thomas "Stonewall" Jackson. Jackson's men were dubbed "foot cavalry" because they would march so fast and so far that it seemed as if they had traveled by horse. Betsy kept up even though her feet, like those of the rest of Jackson's men, were sore and blistered.

When the fighting began, she followed the men onto the field of battle with the regular trappings of a vivandière: water, bandages, lint to pack wounds and help stop bleeding, and some form of painkiller such as whiskey. At one small battle, when a soldier from her hometown fell, she accompanied his body all the way to the train station and home then turned immediately around to rejoin her husband and his regiment.

In 1862, the First Tennessee was transferred from the battlefields of Virginia to the Tennessee front. They were present at the Battle of Shiloh, a bloody battle that lasted two days with many killed and no one side claiming victory.

Betsy again would have been treating wounded while dodging gunfire as Union troops lay siege to Corinth, Mississippi. Corinth was hot and dry. Soldiers were forced to dig shallow holes for drinking water. The water was not clean and was mixed with human waste. Soon more than half the Confederate forces were sick. It would have been a horrible place to be, and Betsy easily could have gone home, but she stayed, choosing to endure the hardships so she could continue to bring comfort to the soldiers under her care. Her mere presence would have benefitted many soldiers. When all they saw were soldiers and dust and sickness, having a woman to remind them of their mother would boost their **morale.**

After Corinth, the armies moved northward into Kentucky, and on October 8, 1862, they clashed in a battle at Perryville. The First Tennessee was in the thick of the fighting and had many men killed or wounded—including Betsy's husband, John. John suffered a severe head wound, which Betsy worked hard to bind. To make matters worse, as she sat upon the blood-soaked ground surrounded by the terrible aftermath of battle—dead and dying soldiers and horses, a landscape devastated by exploding cannon shells—she discovered one of their company's officers, Lt. John Wooldridge, had been blinded. She stayed upon the field with these two men who meant so much to her and to the company even though they were surrounded by enemy soldiers.[2]

Lieutenant Wooldridge and John were taken prisoner. Betsy refused to leave John's side, so she was taken as well, and husband and wife were sent to Camp Chase, a prisoner of war camp in Columbus, Ohio.

Prisoner of war camps during the War Between the States were terrible places. Treatment of prisoners was deplorable. There was poor sanitation, insufficient nutrition, little to no new clothing or blankets, poor shelter, and overcrowding. Thousands—on both sides—died. Large cemeteries exist in both the North and the South where the camps once stood.

One of the most notorious camps was the prison near Andersonville, Georgia, run by the Confederacy. However, many camps in the North were just as terrible and were responsible for a similar death toll. As for Camp Chase, Union general Lew Wallace admitted in his memoirs:

> We are in the habit of speaking and thinking of Andersonville as the acme of horrors; it may have been so, indeed, but of this I am certain, Camp Chase was next to it, the difference being that Andersonville was a Confederate hell for the confinement of enemies taken in arms, while Camp Chase was a hell operated by the old government for friends and sworn supporters.[3]

In Camp Chase, captured Confederate soldiers were incarcerated alongside civilians who disagreed with the war. It is likely Betsy would have been set up in a dorm where Northern women who were being held as political prisoners were staying. Or she may have insisted on being, night and day, with the members of the First Tennessee who were held there.

The Southerners were not acclimated to the colder climate of the North, and when winter came, many froze to death or caught cold-related illnesses. Luckily, the two sides were still exchanging prisoners. One side would agree to swap a certain number of prisoners for some of their men being held prisoner in return. In December, John was exchanged and sent back south; Betsy went with him.

This was the end of Betsy's time in the military, for John's injury was severe enough that he was discharged for disability soon after his return.[4] Betsy spent the rest of the war at home, tending to John's wounds.

Confederate prisoners of war in Camp Chase, Ohio, where Betsy was held prisoner with her husband. (National Archives)

A Taste of History

What did Confederate soldiers eat? The women who followed the Confederate army on the march would have eaten what the soldiers ate, and most soldiers received a ration of salted pork, cornmeal, field peas (also known as black-eyed peas or cow peas), and, when they could get it, salt, sugar, rice, peanuts, and coffee. Sometimes beef was provided, but usually the cattle had to be herded into camp and butchered by the soldiers themselves.

One consistent ingredient was cornmeal. Corn was easier to grow and more plentiful in the South than wheat, so the soldiers received lots of it. Accounts from different soldiers describe many

Field peas, peanuts, and corn dodgers on the broken half of a tin canteen. (Photo by the author)

different and inventive ways of cooking cornmeal, from baking it in cornhusks in the ashes of a fire to rolling the dough into a donut form and sticking it on a bayonet or ramrod to roast over the fire. One common way was to make little "Johnny" or "journey" cakes by frying dough in a pan. The little fried cakes were dubbed "corn dodgers" and could be carried around for days in a haversack and munched on during the march. The little corn cakes would have been familiar to the soldiers as this way of frying cornmeal in a pan dates back to the American Revolution and perhaps even hundreds of years earlier, to the Native American tribes. It is this technique that is included here for you to try.

Ingredients
1 cup cornmeal
1 tsp. salt
1 cup water
2 tbsp. bacon grease

Begin by mixing dry ingredients together in a bowl. Bring water to a boil. (Hint: heat more than 1 cup in case you need more.) In a skillet, heat bacon grease (you can also use lard or butter). Once water has reached a boil, remove saucepan from heat and slowly add water to the dry ingredients. Mix in water a little at a time until you have pliable dough that is not sticky. Form dough into small pancakes about 2 inches in diameter. Place the cakes into the hot grease and cook until bottom side turns a nice golden color then flip and cook the other side until golden. When done, remove to a paper towel to soak up grease. Once they are cool enough to touch, you can eat them. They are best when eaten hot but will keep for several days and can be eaten cold.

Chapter 14

Rose K. Rooney

Louisiana's Irish Rose

Rose was born on the Emerald Isle. Life was hard there in Ireland and people were starving, so while just a teen, she sailed by herself across the ocean to a new home and future in America. She came to the noisy, colorful city of New Orleans. Through that hustle and bustle, where people spoke in French, German, and Spanish, she found a young man to marry. Together they had a family, but a quiet mother Rose was not destined to be. During the "epidemic summer" of 1853, when nearly 8,000 people in the city died of yellow fever, Rose was again left alone. When the drumbeats of 1861 called out to Rose's adventurous spirit, she had no one to care for at home and she set out to be of use in the coming war.

There were many men who answered the call to be soldiers and many units were raised around the city. Women would bring food and gifts to the soldiers as they trained, but not many dared to approach a group of rowdy immigrant firemen who called themselves the Crescent City Blues. They were always getting into trouble, but Rose didn't care. Since no one wanted to show these German, Irish, and French misfits kindness, Rose decided to step up to the task. After all, they were going to risk their lives for their new country and that was enough for Rose.

The men of the Crescent City Blues were happy to have Rose. Already fifty years old, she became much like a mother to the young men and when it was time for them to load onto trains for the war in Virginia, they gave Rose a uniform and insisted she join them.

Rose became an official member of the unit and was off on another adventure.[1] But war, she discovered, was hard. She marched alongside her soldiers, mile after mile, spent nights in the rain, and slept in a drafty tent.

On July 21, 1861, the Crescent City Blues fought in a great battle in Manassas, Virginia. Rose was there. At one point, another unit from New Orleans, the Washington Artillery, was trying to position their cannons on the field so that they could help, but a fence was about to slow down the horses pulling the artillery. Rose rushed out in front of the galloping horses and began tearing down the fence so the cannon could rumble through.

At another battle in 1862, in the town of Fredericksburg, Rose positioned herself in a cemetery just behind the lines. There she nursed the wounded. When Union cannon began to fire at the small field hospital, Rose was urged to leave but she stayed, refusing to abandon the wounded soldiers.

While in camp, she cooked for the men, helped mend their clothes, and tended to them when they were sick as if they were all her adopted sons. Her skirt was riddled with bullets at Gettysburg yet she continued on with her self-proclaimed duty to help wounded soldiers. Rose bravely followed her unit as food became scarce for the Confederate soldiers and her once splendid uniform was reduced to rags. She sat in the muddy trenches at Petersburg and when it was time to surrender at Appomattox, many of the rowdy Crescent City Blues still had the spirit to refuse. Many were arrested, and Rose was with them.

A depiction of Rose removing fence rails to make way for artillery at the First Battle of Manassas.

While she was under guard, one Union officer, not liking Rose's devotion to the Confederacy, asked her about the way Northern soldiers had been treated in Southern prisons. Rose immediately answered, "And what do you have to say about how you treat our poor boys?" The officer only replied by rudely telling her to "shut up."

Rose decided to do just that. Even when she was later questioned, she refused to speak. She was then told to make her own way back to New Orleans, which she soon did.[2]

After the war, Rose continued to help the soldiers. She became head of a soldiers' home, a place for old and sick veterans. There, she worked until she could work no more and took a little room at the home where veterans, old and gray, would come and visit her. They would sit, sharing stories about the adventurous days during the war many years ago.

An unknown Confederate vivandière—and the only known photograph of one in service—distributing from her keg to Zouaves in a New Orleans unit. (Library of Congress)

Women on Battlefields: A History

For centuries, women have played a role on battlefields, though not as combatants. Many women followed their husbands and sons across battlefields of Europe as cooks, nurses, and seamstresses. Before the eighteenth century, lords and members of the nobility paid for their own armies. Since armies were not raised by a central government, the clothing, food, and care of the soldiers were left to their family members.

Historically there were few schools women could attend in order to learn medicine and receive training as a doctor. Therefore, most healing was done by older women who had learned medicine from their mothers, who had learned their skills from their own mothers. Until becoming a physician required schooling in a university, women were the main caregivers and were needed to tend the soldiers.

By the time of the War Between the States (1861-1865), governments were firmly in charge of armies and they paid businesses to do what women had traditionally done. Medical schools were also started for men to become doctors, but women were not allowed to attend. These changes meant fewer women worked with the armies.

Some governments, such as France, still saw women as being important to the military in the roles of caregivers, nurses, mascots, and mother figures. (Men act better if they have someone like a mom around!) In fact the French military in the 1860s actually required that each regiment employ a certain number of women. They called these women **vivandières** (viv-on-dee-ays), which means "caregiver" in French.

When war broke out in America in 1861, there were many people in both the North and the South who had recently come from Europe. As the Union and Confederate armies were raised, many of the soldiers wanted vivandières in their new units. Usually there was a soldier's daughter, wife, or mother who volunteered to help care for the soldiers and act as a vivandière. When it was time to go to war, the men agreed to buy her a feminine version of their uniform and invited her to join them.

Most of the vivandières, like Kady Brownell, only remained with the regiment for the first year of the war before going home. It was tough living with the army. The women had to march many miles, sleep in tents in very cold and very hot weather, eat bad food, and sometimes be exposed to the dangers of battle. Some women did stay for the duration of the war, but it is difficult to say how many, as they were usually not listed on official documents.

Overall, the number of women who served as daughters of the regiment or vivandières is uncertain. Uncovering their stories is an ongoing process. In the North, many of their stories were put into books and some women wrote down their stories in journals. In the South, far fewer of the women's stories were recorded as after the war they were more focused on rebuilding or simply surviving in a land where their homes and farms had been destroyed. It is only through records and wartime accounts in letters that their stories can be found. For example, a wartime paper gives the following account of an event in Memphis:

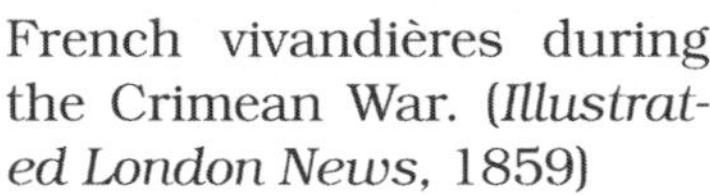

French vivandières during the Crimean War. (*Illustrated London News*, 1859)

Arrest of a New Orleans Vivandiere.

It seems that some of the Louisiana Regiments have vivandieres attached to them, and their services in Virginia have been spoken of in the highest terms. One of these devoted women, named Helen Voskius, of about twenty years, who accompanied her regiment to Virginia, arrived here yesterday. Her hair was plaited, and her jaunty cap, bloomer pants and close fitting coat, rendered her the observed of all observes [*sic*]. Everybody could see that she was a woman, and some of our police, not being acquainted with such a uniform for the gentler sex, arrested her. She was taken to the station house, the matter explained and Capt. Klink at once set her at liberty. We are sorry that the lovely vivandiere should have been incommoded, and on the part of our citizens generally beg leave to offer our best apology.[1]

In another account, a soldier who served with the Washington Artillery, a Confederate unit out of New Orleans, wrote:

"Mistress John," his [John Bahr's] *frau*, whom Slocomb had uniformed as a *vivandière* before leaving home, accompanied us, and bore the fatigue of the campaigns as well as any. She made herself indispensable in many ways. The little woman was a heroine in her way, as true as steel; and many a sick or wounded fellow has felt her motherly hand as she bated his hurt or made for him a good broth or a cup of creole coffee. The boys, always ready for *sobriquets*, dubbed the worthy couple [Mr. and Mrs. John Bahr], more from affection than from any disrespect, the "he-bear and the she-bear"; and so they were known for the term of the war.[2]

The gravestone for Rebecca Sineath in Magnolia Cemetery near Morris Island, South Carolina. (Courtesy of Hugh McLaren)

One must keep a sharp eye out, as sometimes the evidence of these women's service will come by surprise. A walk through Magnolia Cemetery in South Carolina has a Veterans Affairs Confederate headstone that reads: "Rebecca Sineath, Laundress for the 21st SC Infantry, Born 1846, Died June 19, 1863, Morris Island, SC."

Records of the time reveal that she died of typhoid, along with many of the soldiers in the regiment, and that she was carefully laid to rest separately from the soldiers under the shade of a tree. She had been orphaned several years earlier and followed a brother who entered the Confederate service as a sergeant. No other information exists to flesh out who she was, but maybe someday, someone will find some old letters or a journal that gives us more insight into her story.

As time passes, how many more heroic stories will be discovered, hiding away in some archive in a museum's back room or a dusty old trunk? Will you find one and tell her story?

A living historian portrays a vivandière at a reenactment in 2017. (Photo by the author)

Glossary

Accoutrements: A soldier's gear or "kit," such as belts, cartridge box, primer pouch, and bayonet, needed for fighting.

Amputate: To remove something, usually a part of the body, through surgery. Due to the way the soft bullets used during the war shattered bone, many soldiers who were hit in an arm or leg had to have the limb amputated. Amputation was the most common procedure done by surgeons during the War Between the States.

Apprentice: When a student wanted to learn a trade, such as in the case of James Cox, who wanted to learn to run a newspaper, he would apprentice himself to someone already working in the trade. The apprentice would act as an assistant and learn how to do the job. Before 1900, working as an apprentice was more common than going to college.

Artillery: Military branch in which the soldiers fire cannon. In the 1860s this could mean large cannon for sieges or "flying artillery," which were smaller cannon pulled by teams of four to six horses.

Auxiliary: An auxiliary position in the military is a supportive role. Soldiers in auxiliary positions did not fight in the battles with rifles, but they completed important jobs that needed to be done in order for the military to run smoothly. Some of these positions were surgeons, nurses, ambulance drivers, blacksmiths, chaplains, and musicians.

Barter: A system where goods or services are exchanged instead of money. Bartering was a frequent practice in early rural America and became more frequent in the South during and after the war as few individuals had any money. For example, a person in need of the services of a doctor might agree to give the doctor a chicken for payment.

Blockade: During the war, the Union sent ships to block all the harbors and ports around the South in an attempt to prevent all trade between the Confederacy and foreign countries such as Britain, France, Brazil, and Spanish Cuba, who quietly supported the South. The South created fast ships called "blockade runners" that would attempt to outrun the Union vessels guarding the ports at sea.

Campaign: When an army is on the march and fighting battles with little rest.

Carpetbagger: A term Southerners gave to Northerners who came down after the war to abuse the people and property for their own personal profit.

Cartridge Box: A leather box that either hung on a strap that went over and across the shoulder or on a belt. It was opened by a flap and contained cartridges—powder and bullets—for firing a rifle or musket. Usually around sixty rounds could be held in a cartridge box.

Casualty: A soldier who has been killed, wounded, or taken prisoner as a result of a battle. Civilians who are wounded or killed due to a war are also considered casualties. New estimates for the total number of people killed during the War Between the States have reached as high as 800,000. For many years, historians estimated the number at 620,000, but that figure did not include Southern civilians nor many soldiers who died from their wounds after the close of the war.

Cavalry: Soldiers who fight from horseback. These mounted soldiers were used for scouting out enemy positions or raiding because they could cover ground quickly. By the 1860s, it was rare for cavalry to attack soldiers on foot during battle.

Citizen: Someone who holds allegiance to a specific government. Prior to the Fourteenth Amendment, citizenship in America was defined in relation to each individual state. So individuals were citizens of the state in which they lived, not the United States.

Civil War: See War Between the States.

Color-Bearer: The soldier who carries a unit's flag. Flags carried by soldiers in battle are called the unit's "colors."

Daughter of the Regiment: A woman who is adopted as a mascot of a military regiment. Some may have never strayed far from home and only marched with the unit for parades, but others accompanied the men and endured all of the same hardships.

Desert: To leave the army without permission, usually with no intention of coming back. If a soldier ran away from the army, he was called a deserter and if caught, he could be tried before a military court and sentenced to death by firing squad or hanging.

Disenfranchise: To take away someone's right to participate in government. Some ways to disenfranchise a person include taking away their right to vote, run for office, or serve on a jury. Former Confederate soldiers were disenfranchised after the war unless they took a loyalty oath to the United States. Since many Confederates saw the oath as requiring them to be a traitor to their state, they did not want to say it.

Enlist: To join or sign up for the military. Enlisting usually means that the individual is joining voluntarily rather than being "drafted" or forced to join.

Espionage: Spying. Someone accused of espionage could be a hired spy or a citizen who accidentally overheard valuable information from the enemy that they then decided to share with their own side.

Field Hospital: A temporary hospital set up in a tent or house close to a battle to treat the wounded.

Hardtack: A hard cracker or biscuit made from flour, water, and salt and eaten by soldiers.

Infantry: Soldiers who march and fight on foot. During the nineteenth century, they carried long rifles or muskets and fought in tightly packed formations.

Latrine: Ditches soldiers used as restrooms.

Military Hospital: During the War Between the States, most military hospitals were temporary hospitals set up in large buildings in cities. Many hotels were taken over by the military for use as a hospital for convalescing soldiers.

Militia: An organization of civilians who would perform military training outside of a war. It was extremely common prior to the 1860s and was looked upon as a source of reserve troops by the federal government. Militia even had an accepted uniform color in both the North and the South: gray. When the war began in 1861, since most of the Confederate troops originated from militia, the color gray was adopted as the standard uniform color for the Confederacy while the standard color for regular federal troops was blue, which became the color for all Union uniforms.

Minié Ball: Bullets used in most of the rifles during the war. They were cone shaped, .58 caliber, and made of soft lead. They were far more accurate than the old musket balls and caused terrible damage to anyone who was unlucky enough to be wounded by them. Rifles using the bullets were long and loaded one bullet at a time through the muzzle. The most common rifles that fired the Minié balls were the model 1861 Springfield, made in Massachusetts for the Union, and the 1853 Enfield, made in England and shipped to the Confederacy.

Morale: The general feeling or mood of the soldiers. In the military, a soldier's or army's morale is important. Soldiers who are happy and confident of victory are easier to lead. Soldiers whose morale is low are sad, even angry, and have a propensity for running away or getting into trouble.

Presentism: The act of placing modern thoughts and morals on people of the past. A good historian avoids presentism, understanding that people of the past thought and understood things somewhat differently than we do today. For example, what is considered very wrong today—such as keeping a slave or burning someone for being a witch—was accepted or even moral to people of the past. We should not judge people of the past by our modern standards because how do we know we would not have acted the same had we lived in their time?

Reconstruction: A period of twelve years (1865-1877) after the war during which the Southern states were not allowed back into the Union until they performed certain tasks that showed they would obey the government in Washington, D.C. The South was ruled by the military and sectioned into five military districts overseen by a general. During this time, many opportunistic Northern businessmen came to the South and bought up land and raised taxes. Many families had to sell what little they had left to pay them. It was a difficult time for people of all races in the South. Many former slaves fled North since their homes were gone too, and the more adventurous went west. (One-third of cowboys were black.) Many white Southerners fled west to Texas or California or even overseas. For those who stayed, it took more than one hundred years to rebuild. The effects of the war can still be seen today, as before the war Louisiana was the richest state in the nation; now it is one of the poorest.

Rheumatism: A common ailment during the war and known today as rheumatic fever. This illness is caused by a combination of the untreated strep virus and a lack of vitamin C. The soldiers' poor nutrition during winter coupled with the highly contagious nature of strep throat would allow the virus to develop into scarlet fever and then rheumatic fever, which is characterized by a rash, fever, and swollen joints. A third of those who suffer lasting effects experience swollen, painful joints and even heart damage.

Secede: To separate from politically. The Southern states seceded from the Union, meaning they separated themselves from the United States.

Sharpshooter: A soldier who is very skilled at shooting a rifle. Both armies had special sharpshooting regiments or battalions. The modern term "sniper" was not yet known or used in America in the 1860s.

Subject: An individual who holds allegiance to a nation that has a king or queen. America's original colonists were subjects. After the American Revolution, Americans became citizens while those in Britain or British colonies remained subjects.

Sutler: A person who runs a makeshift store in a military camp. They sold goods that were not provided as regular rations to the soldiers, such as condensed milk, fru its, vegetables, jams, butter, smoked meat, eggs and cheese from local farms, newspapers, books, sewing supplies, shaving razors, soap, tooth powder, ink, paper, tobacco, and sometimes alcohol and medicine.

Vivandière: French term meaning "caregiver." The French army instituted vivandières as an official position in their military. Some of the regiments raised during the War Between the States mimicked this practice.

War Between the States: The official name for the American Civil War. Congress recognized this title for the conflict in 1928. Using the term "War Between the States" when studying world history helps prevent confusion between the American Civil War and the civil wars of other countries.

Washington City: During the nineteenth century, Washington, D.C. was called Washington City.

Notes

Chapter 1

1. "Honor Is Her Due: Mrs. Brownell, Heroine of Bull Run and Newbern," *Saturday Globe* (Utica, NY), December 21, 1895.
2. "At the Universalist," *The Daily Northwestern* (Oshkosh, WI), November 28, 1892.
3. Frank Moore, *Women of the War* (Harford, CT: S. S. Scranton, and Co., 1866), 22.
4. Moore, 24.

Chapter 2

1. L.P. Brockett and Mary C. Vaughn, *Woman's Work in the Civil War: A Record of Heroism, Patriotism, and Patience* (Philadelphia: Zeigler, McCurdy and Co., 1867), 147-53.
2. Philip N. Racine, ed. *"Unspoiled Heart": The Journal of Charles Mattocks of the 17th Maine* (Knoxville: University of Tennessee Press, 1994).
3. Elizabeth D. Leonard, *All the Daring of a Soldier* (New York: W. W. Norton Company, 1999), 111.

Chapter 3

1. Susie King Taylor, *Reminiscences of My Life in Camp With the 33rd United States Colored Troops Late 1st S.C. Volunteers* (Boston: Published by the Author, 1902), http://docsouth.unc.edu/neh/taylorsu/taylorsu.html. Most of the information that exists on Susie Baker can be taken directly from her memoirs that she wrote after the war.
2. Record pulled from National Archives and compiled with other Confederates of color in Ricardo J. Rodriguez's *Black Confederates in the U.S. Civil War: A Complete List of African-Americans Who Served the Confederacy* (San Antonio, Texas: Ricardo, 2010).

Chapter 4

1. Bernhard Tape (Private, 27th Pennsylvania Infantry), "Indexes to the Carded Records of Soldiers Who Served in Volunteer Organizations During the Civil War, compiled 1899-1927, documenting the period 1861-1866," National Archives. M554. Group 4. Roll 121.

Chapter 5

1. Dale L. Walker, *Mary Edwards Walker: Above and Beyond* (New York: MacMillan, 2005).
2. Richard H. Hall, *Women on the Civil War Battlefront* (Lawrence, KS: University Press of Kansas, 2006), 149.

Chapter 6

1. "Heroic Women at the Cannons Mouth in the Civil War," published in the *Oregonian* on June 4, 1911, ran a story by a veteran who told a story of Bridget's husband being wounded and how she grabbed her cap and exclaimed in an Irish brogue that she would "Avenge me husband!" However, the First Michigan was not present at the battle the veteran referenced, Fair Oaks, on October 1862. Either the veteran did not recall the correct battle or he had witnessed another woman on the field. William Devere's record in the National Archives shows desertion in November of 1862.
2. E. F. Conklin, *Women at Gettysburg: 1863* (Gettysburg, PA: Thomas Publications, 1993), 139.
3. Charlotte Elizabeth McKay, *Stories of Hospital and Camp* (Philadelphia: Claxton, Remson, & Haffelfinger, 1876).
4. Mary A. Livermore, *My Story of the War: Woman's Narrative of Four Years Personal Experience as Nurse in the Union Army, and at Relief Work at Home, in Hospitals, Camps, and at the Front During the War of the Rebellion* (Hartford, CT: A.D. Worthington and Company, 1888).
5. Conklin, *Women at Gettysburg*, 142.

Chapter 7

1. Matthew Page Andrews, *The Women of the South in War Times* (Baltimore, MD: Norman, Remington, 1924), 127.
2. Andrews, *The Women of the South*, 128.

Chapter 8

1. Susan Matthis Johnson, "Will the Real Nancy Hart Come Forth," *The Hur Herald* (Richwood, WV), July 23, 2016. The *Hur Herald*, a news site based in Hart's West Virginia hometown, has done research on Nancy Hart for years using not only the few printed sources in existence but also interviewing Nancy Hart's grandchildren. The *Hur Herald* also researches local lore dealing with the war and the Moccasin Rangers.
2. Ibid.
3. Marion H. Kerner, "The Lady Guerilla and the Telegrapher." *Leslie's Weekly*, May 26, 1910. Marion H. Kerner was a telegrapher with Colonel Starr who witnessed the capture of Nancy Hart and helped as she was photographed. He sold his story to *Leslie's Weekly*, where it was published in 1910.

Chapter 9

1. Mary Sophia Hill, *A British Subject's Recollection of the Confederacy While a Visitor and Attendant in Its Hospitals and Camps*, trans. by the Louisiana Division of the UDC (Baltimore Turnbull Brothers, 1875). Most of the information on

Mary Sophia Hill is taken from her diary, which was recently transcribed and launched digitally by the Louisiana Division of the United Daughters of the Confederacy.

Chapter 10

1. Information on Sindy Riller can be found in the Kaufman County Commissioners records. Record of the $38 was recorded in January 1865.

Chapter 11

1. Michelle A. Krowl, "Cox, Lucy Ann White," in *Dictionary of Virginia Biography*, vol. 3, ed. by Sara B. Bearss (Richmond: Library of Virginia, 2006), 512.
2. "Col. W. R. Aylett's Address before Pickett Camp," *Star* (Richmond, VA), July 21, 1894.
3. James A. Cox (Private, 30th Virginia). "Carded Records Showing Military Service of Soldiers Who Fought in Confederate Organizations, compiled 1903-1927, documenting the period 1861-1865." *National Archives*. M324. Group 9. Roll 732.

Chapter 12

1. Oriana Moon to Gen. John H. Cocke, July 19, 1861, Cocke Family Papers, Special Collections, Alderman Library, University of Virginia.
2. Scottsville Museum, "Dr. Oriana Moon, A Confederate Doctor," last modified 2001, https://scottsvillemuseum.com/war/moon/home.html.

Chapter 13

1. Andrews, *The Women of the South*, 113.
2. Ibid. 114-15.
3. Lew, Wallace, *Smoke, Sound, & Fury: The Civil War Memoirs of Major-General Lew Wallace, U.S. Volunteers* (Madison, WI: University of Wisconsin, 1998), 173.
4. Sullivan, John (Private, 1st Tennessee, Co. K). "Carded Records Showing Military Service of Soldiers Who Fought in Confederate Organizations, compiled 1903-1927, documenting the period 1861-1865." National Archives. M268. Group 9. Roll 105.

Chapter 14

1. Rooney, Rose K. (Laundress, 15th Louisiana). "Carded Records Showing Military Service of Soldiers Who Fought in Confederate Organizations, compiled 1903-1927, documenting the period 1861-1865." *National Archives*. M320. Group 9. Roll 271.
2. Fannie A. Beers, *Memories: A Record of Personal Experience and Adventure during Four Years of War* (Philadelphia: J.B. Lippincott, 1888), 217-20.

Women in Battlefields: A History

1. "Arrest of a New Orleans Vivandiere," *The Daily Dispatch* (Richmond, VA), September 19, 1861.
2. William Miller Owen, *In Camp and Battle with the Washington Artillery of New Orleans* (Boston: Ticknor and Company, 1885; Baton Rouge: Louisiana State University Press, 1999), 21.

Bibliography

Andrews, Matthew Page. *The Women of the South in War Times.* Baltimore, MD: Norman, Remington, 1924.

"Arrest of a New Orleans Vivandiere." *The Daily Dispatch* (Richmond, VA), September 19, 1861.

"At the Universalist." *The Daily Northwestern* (Oshkosh, WI), November 28, 1892.

Bakeless, John Edwin. *Spies of the Confederacy.* Philadelphia: J. B. Lippincott, 1970.

Bauer, Crickett. "Viva la Vivandières: A Short History of Women in Pseudo-Military Costume." *Military Images* XXI, no. 20 (May/June 2000): 20-24.

Beers, Fannie A. *Memories: A Record of Personal Experience and Adventure during Four Years of War.* Philadelphia: J.B. Lippincott, 1888.

Brockett, L.P., and Mary C. Vaughn. *Woman's Work in the Civil War: A Record of Heroism, Patriotism, and Patience.* Philadelphia: Zeigler, McCurdy and Co., 1867.

Brooks, Ross. "Red Petticoats and Blue Jackets: 1st Confederate States Zouave Battalion or Coppens' Louisiana Zouaves," *Military Collector and Historian* XLV, no. 4 (winter, 1993).

Canon, Jill. *Civil War Heroines.* Santa Barbara, CA: Bellerophon Books, 2000.

"Col. W. R. Aylett's Address before Pickett Camp." *Star* (Richmond, VA), July 21, 1894.

Conklin, E. F. *Women at Gettysburg: 1863.* Gettysburg, PA: Thomas Publications, 1993.

Cox, James A. (Private, 30th Virginia). "Carded Records Showing Military Service of Soldiers Who Fought in Confederate Organizations, compiled 1903-1927, documenting the period 1861-1865." *National Archives.* M324. Group 9. Roll 732.

Cumming, Kate. *Kate: The Journal of a Confederate Nurse.* Baton Rouge: LSU Press, 1998.

Davis, Curtis Carroll, ed. *Belle Boyd in Camp and Prison, Written by Herself.* New York: Thomas Yoseloff, 1968.

Davis, Curtis Carroll. "Effie Goldsborough: Confederate Courier." *Civil War Times Illustrated* 7 (April 1968): 29-31.

Devere, William. (Private, 1st Michigan Cavalry, Co. I). "Organization Index to Pension Files of Veterans Who Served Between 1861 and 1900, compiled 1949-1949, documenting the period 1861-942." *National Archives.* T289. Group 5. Roll pub57.

Grefe, C. Morgan, Ph.D., Executive Director, Rhode Island Historical Society. "Kady Southwell Brownell (1843-1915)." North Burial Ground Project. http://www.rice.edu/northburialground/tours_women-BrownellKady.html.

Hacker, Barton C. "Women and Military Institutions in Early Modern Europe: A Reconnaissance." *Signs* 6, no. 4 (summer, 1981): 643-71.

Hall, Richard H. *Women on the Civil War Battlefront.* Lawrence, KS: University Press of Kansas, 2006.

Hennessey, James. "The Vivandieres of the Louisiana Zouave Battalion." *Journal, Confederate Historical Society of Great Britain* 17, no. 1 (spring 1989), 2-3.

"Heroic Women at the Cannons Mouth in the Civil War." *Oregonian* (Portland, OR), June 4, 1911.

Hill, Mary Sophia. *A British Subject's Recollection of the Confederacy While a Visitor and Attendant in Its Hospitals and Camps.* Transcribed by the Louisiana Division of the UDC. Baltimore: Turnbull Brothers, 1875.

Holland, Mary Gardner. *Our Army Nurses.* Roseville, MN: Edinborough Press, 1998.

"Honor Is Her Due: Mrs. Brownell, Heroine of Bull Run and Newbern." *Saturday Globe* (Utica, NY), December 21, 1895.

Jessee, Gail R. "Origins of Confederate Cantinieres." *United Daughters of the Confederacy Magazine* 58, no. 1 (Jan. 1995): 15.

Johnson, Susan Matthis. "Will the Real Nancy Hart Come Forth." *The Hur Herald* (Richwood, WV), July 23, 2016.

Kerner, Marion H. "The Lady Guerilla and the Telegrapher." *Leslie's Weekly*, May 26, 1910.

Krowl, Michelle A. "Cox, Lucy Ann White." In *Dictionary of Virginia Biography.* Vol. 3, edited by Sara B. Bearss, 512-13. Richmond: Library of Virginia, 2006.

Laffin, John. *Women in Battle.* New York: Aberlard-Schuman, 1967.

Leonard, Elizabeth D. *All the Daring of a Soldier.* New York: W. W. Norton Company, 1999.

———. "To 'Don the Breeches, and Slay Them with a Will!' A Host of Women Soldiers." In *The Civil War Soldier*, 69-81. New York: NYU Press, 2002.

Livermore, Mary A. *My Story of the War: Woman's Narrative of Four Years Personal Experience as Nurse in the Union Army, and at Relief Work at Home, in Hospitals, Camps, and at the Front During the War of the Rebellion.* Hartford, CT: A.D. Worthington and Company, 1888.

Massey, Mary Elizabeth. *Bonnet Brigades.* New York: Alfred A. Knopf, 1966.

McKay, Charlotte Elizabeth. *Stories of Hospital and Camp.* Philadelphia: Claxton, Remson, & Haffelfinger, 1876.

McPherson, James M. *For Cause & Comrades: Why Men Fought in the Civil War.* New York: Oxford University Press, 1997.

Mills, H. Sinclair. *The Vivandiere: History, Tradition, Uniform and Service.* Collinswood, NJ: Civil War Historicals, 1988.

Moore, Frank. *Women of the War.* Harford, CT: S. S. Scranton, and Co., 1866.

Mylott, Jim. "County History: The Story of Nancy Hart." *The Times Record* (Spencer, WV), May 10, 1979.

Owen, William Miller. *In Camp and Battle with the Washington Artillery of New Orleans.* Boston: Ticknor and Company, 1885. Reprint, Baton Rouge: LSU Press, 1999.

Racine, Philip N., ed. *"Unspoiled Heart": The Journal of Charles Mattocks of the 17th Maine.* Knoxville: University of Tennessee Press, 1994.

"Rhome Woman, 94, is Typical Pioneer." *Wise County Messenger* (Wise County, TX), July 31, 1938.

Rodriguez, Ricardo J. *Black Confederates in the U.S. Civil War: A Complete List of African-Americans Who Served the Confederacy.* San Antonio, TX: Ricardo, 2010.

Rooney, Rose K. (Laundress, 15th Louisiana). "Carded Records Showing Military Service of Soldiers Who Fought in Confederate Organizations, compiled 1903-1927, documenting the period 1861-1865." *National Archives.* M320. Group 9. Roll 271.

Scottsville Museum. "Dr. Oriana Moon, A Confederate Doctor." Last modified 2001. https://scottsvillemuseum.com/war/moon/home.html.

Sullivan, John (Private, 1st Tennessee, Co. K). "Carded Records Showing Military Service of Soldiers Who Fought in Confederate Organizations, compiled 1903-1927, documenting the period 1861-1865." National Archives. M268. Group 9. Roll 105.

Swearnigin, Ben (Private, 12th Texas Cavalry). "Carded Records Showing Military Service of Soldiers Who Fought in Confederate Organizations, compiled 1903-1927, documenting the period 1861-1865." National Archives. M323. Group 9. Roll 074.

Tape, Bernhard. (Private, 27th Pennsylvania Infantry). "Indexes to the Carded Records of Soldiers Who Served in Volunteer Organizations During the Civil War, compiled 1899-1927, documenting the period 1861-1866." National Archives. M554. Group 4. Roll 121.

Taylor, Susie King. *Reminiscences of My Life in Camp With the 33rd United States Colored Troops Late 1st S.C. Volunteers.* Boston: Published by the Author, 1902. http://docsouth.unc.edu/neh/taylorsu/taylorsu.html.

Walker, Dale L. *Mary Edwards Walker: Above and Beyond.* New York: MacMillan, 2005.

Wallace, Lew. *Smoke, Sound, & Fury: The Civil War Memoirs of Major-General Lew Wallace, U.S. Volunteers.* Madison, WI: University of Wisconsin, 1998.

The War of the Rebellion: A Compilation of the Official Records of the Union and Confederate Armies. 130 volumes. Washington, D.C.: Government Printing Office, 1880-1901.

Wiley, Bell Irvin. *Confederate Women.* Westport, CT: Greenwood Press, 1975.

"Woman Veteran of the Civil War." *Saturday Globe* (Utica, NY), January 16, 1915.

Wood, Leonora. *Belle Boyd: Famous Spy of the Confederate States Army.* Keyser, WV: Mountain Echo, 1940.

Wooldridge, John H. (Sergeant/Lieutenant, 1st Tennessee [Field's]). "Carded Records Showing Military Service of Soldiers Who Fought in Confederate Organizations, compiled 1903-1927, documenting the period 1861-1865." *National Archives.* M260. Group 9. Roll 105.

Index

Alcott, Louisa May, 24
amputation, 66, 86
Arkansas, 62

Baker, Susie, 26-29
Barton, Clara, 24
Bickerdyke, Mary Ann, 24
blockade, 50, 62
Boles, Sindy Riller, 9, 61-62
Boyd, Belle, 46, 54
Brownell, Kady, 15-18
Bull Run (Manassas), Battle of, 16, 21, 23, 64, 69-71, 80

Camp Chase Prison, 75-76
Chimborazo Hospital, 66
Corinth, Battle of, 75
Cox, Lucy Ann, 64-67
Custer, Gen. George A., 41-43

Davis, Pres. Jefferson, 29, 48-49, 54
Divers, Bridget, 41-42, 44, 56

espionage, 38, 46, 53-54, 58
Etheridge, Annie, 20-21, 23-24

field hospital, 21, 24, 32, 34, 37, 42, 57, 60, 65

Gettysburg, Battle of, 12, 21, 32, 35, 43, 80
Grant, Gen. Ulysses S., 21, 33, 66

Hart, Nancy, 52-53
Hill, Mary Sophia, 55-58
hospital, 21, 24, 28, 37, 40, 48-49, 58, 65-66, 71, 80

Jackson, Gen. Thomas "Stonewall", 29, 74

Kearny, Gen. Philip, 21
Kentucky, 75

laundress, 57, 74, 84
Lee, Gen. Robert E., 66
Lincoln, Pres. Abraham, 64
Louisiana, 53, 57-58, 63, 79, 84

medicine, 21, 31, 42, 45, 49-51, 62
Michigan, 20, 41
Mississippi, 75
Moon, Lottie, 69-70, 72
Moon, Oriana, 69-70, 73
Mosby, Col. John S., 42

New Orleans, 57-58, 79-81, 84
nurse, 21, 24, 26, 28, 34, 37, 40, 48, 58, 68, 82

Ohio, 12, 38, 75-76

Pennsylvania, 19, 28, 30-32, 69
Perryville, Battle of, 75

Reconstruction, 68
Rhode Island, 15-16
Rooney, Rose, 79-80

Sharpsburg (Antietam), Battle of, 21, 23, 65
Shiloh (Pittsburg Landing), Battle of, 23, 75
slavery, 26-27, 29, 48, 52, 55, 63, 69-70, 72
smuggling, 58-59
spies. see espionage
Sullivan, Betsy, 74-76
surgeon, 24, 34, 37-38, 57, 69-70, 72-73, 86
surgery, 37, 86

taxes, 72
Tennessee, 54, 72, 74-75
Tepe, Mary, 30, 33, 41
Texas, 61-63, 68
Tompkins, Capt. Sally, 48-49

Virginia, 16, 21, 32, 37-38, 40, 46, 48, 52, 57-58, 60, 64-66, 69-70, 73-75, 79-80, 84
vivandière, 9-10, 18, 31, 33, 45, 67, 75, 81, 84-85

Walker, Dr. Mary, 36-39
Wallace, Gen. Lew, 76

Zouaves, 30-31, 34